REVELATION
The Time Is Near

Dr. Billy J. Owensby

Library of Congress Control Number: 2021923836
ISBN-13:   Paperback: 978-1-64749-657-9
             Epub: 978-1-64749-658-6

Printed in the United States of America

GoToPublish LLC
1-888-337-1724
www.gotopublish.com
info@gotopublish.com

CONTENTS

REVELATION
(INTRODUCTION)

This is one of the most unique and misunderstood books found in God's Word. There are many individuals who believe that Revelation is a book that is not to be taught thinking it is too difficult to understand. However, we must remember that it is the work of the Holy Spirit to teach the believer truth and also lead him to a greater understanding of the Word of God. Revelation 1:3 states, "Blessed is he who reads and those who hear the words of the prophecy, and heed the things which are written in it; for the time is near." Notice this verse says blessed is the one who <u>reads</u>, <u>hears</u>, and <u>heeds</u> the things written in it. It does not say anything about understanding. Again, be reminded that we have the promise of God's Word that the Holy Spirit will guide us into and teach us all truth.

One of the first decisions that an individual has to make is which interpretive view he will take. There are basically four views regarding the interpretation of the book of the Revelation:

1. **Preterist View** – This view stated in its simplest form says that Revelation relates only to the first century. The author is writing about the events of his own day. This view ignores the issue of prophecy. This view sees the words about the Second Coming of Christ as being fulfilled when the temple was destroyed in A.D. 70.

2. **Historical View** – This view represents and relates to the first century to the present. This view like the Preterist view ignores the fact of prophecy. Revelation in this view is seen as simply an outline of major events.

3. **Idealist/Spiritualist/Symbolic View** – This view is a non-literal interpretation of the book of Revelation. This view takes the approach of the struggle between good and evil.

The author is said to be simply stating spiritual truths and principles. This view also ignores the fact of prophecy.

4. **Futurist View** – This view sees Revelation 4-22 as events which are yet to take place. This view relates to the end times. The messages to the seven churches in Chapters 1 through 3 is said to be an exception. Almost every interpreter says that a historical background is seen in these churches. Some see the seven churches as representing different church ages, leading up to the end time. The futurist view takes Revelation to be a book of prophecy and shows the book to be a picture of future events.

Author:

The author identifies himself as John in the book four different times (**1:1, 4, 9; 22:8**). There are many words used in the Revelation that are used by John the disciple in the Gospel of John and the Epistles of John. The early church was very much in agreement that John a disciple of Jesus Christ, the son of Zebedee, was the author of Revelation.

Date:

The writing of Revelation was perhaps around A.D. 95-96. This would have been during the time of the Domitian reign. Some hold to an earlier date of A.D. 68 at which time Nero would be in power. The later date seems to carry greater evidence as one looks at the circumstances and also conditions of the churches to which John was writing.

Finally, Revelation is a book of numbers and a book of symbols. Numbers and symbols are representative of a truth being given to the readers. Being under great persecution the Christian readers would understand and know that the Apostle John was relaying a message in what might be considered to be a spiritual code. The readers of the day would find great encouragement and motivation for living a righteous and holy life.

THE REVELATION OF JESUS CHRIST
REVELATION 1:1-6

I. The Person of The Book (1a)
1. This book is the Revelation of Jesus Christ.
    A) Revelation (apokalupsis) – To become visible, unveiling, to reveal, pull back a covering.
    B) Jesus came to earth as a babe in a manger with His glory veiled. He will come again with His glory unveiled.
    C) One must be careful not to separate the Person of Jesus from the prophecy of the book.
    D) Jesus is the Chief Person of the Revelation and without Him there would be no prophecy to fulfill.
    E) In Revelation we see Jesus receive the sealed scroll which is the title deed of the earth, His inheritance.
2. Revelation simply put is all about Jesus!

II. The Purpose of The Book (1b)
1. "To show to His bond-servants, the things which must soon take place…"
    A) Soon (tachos) – in a brief time.
    B) The Tribulation Period and judgment are soon to come.
    C) The soon coming of Jesus Christ.
    D) The saints undergoing persecution would find encouragement and motivation to live holy lives.
2. Bond-Servants
    A) (Doulois) – slaves
    B) These were God's servants who served Him being compelled by their love for Him.
3. Christians today need to be reminded that Christ could return at any moment and the time of the Tribulation Period could begin these future events of the Revelation.

———

1

III. The Pattern of The Book (1c)

1. "And He sent and _communicated_ it…" (NASB)
2. "And He sent and _signified_ it…" (KJV)
3. Communicated or Signified
   A) To give a sign or symbol.
   B) "Signified" is a word used by many scholars.
   C) This is true because it is a book of signs and symbols.
4. This makes Revelation a unique book because it is the only New Testament book communicated to a human author by angels.
5. Often times symbols or signs may speak more accurately because words change, symbols do not.
   A) Stars – messengers
   B) Lamps – churches
   C) Incense – prayer

IV. The Proclamation of The Book (2)

1. John is proclaiming a prophetic message.
2. The phrase "the Word of God" emphasizes the uniqueness of the message given.
3. The phrase "the testimony of Jesus" is the subject of Revelation and is synonymous with "the Word of God."
4. John faithfully recorded all He was commanded and all that he saw.
5. John Phillips makes a profound statement when he says, "We must be as careful reading the book of Revelation as John was recording it."

V. The Promise of The Book (3)

1. A special promise is given regarding the book of Revelation.
2. The verb "read" means to read aloud.
3. The blessing relates to those who also _hears_ the words of this prophecy.

4. The blessing involves not only <u>hearing</u> but <u>heeding</u> the things which are written in it.
5. We today should read, hear, and heed the things of this prophecy and not ignore or neglect the Revelation.
6. **James 1:22-24** "But prove yourselves doers of the word, and not merely hearers who delude them-selves. For if anyone is a hearer of the word and not a doer, he is like man who looks at his natural face in a mirror; for once he has looked at himself and gone away, he has immediately forgotten what kind of person he was."
7. This is the first of seven beatitudes found within the Revelation.

VI. The People Receiving The Letter (4a)
1. Special messages are given to each of the seven churches in Chapters 2-3.
2. These churches in Asia Minor were confronted with and facing great persecution.
3. God begins His message to the churches with grace and peace.
4. Although God's judgment would soon come, His words of grace and peace would be a comfort and an encouragement to them.
5. It should be noted that the seven churches of Asia Minor are typical of churches everywhere and for all times.

VII. The Person Sending The Letter (4b-5a)
1. God The Father (**4**)
   A) "Him who is and who was and who is to come."
   B) This phrase describes God the Father as unchangeable and eternal.
2. God The Holy Spirit (**4**)
   A) "The seven Spirits who are before His throne…"
   B) Seven – completeness, perfection, fullness.

C) It is the Spirit of God who lives within the believer and fills the believer.
3. God The Son (**5**)
    A) Faithful Witness (martyr) [Prophet]
    B) First Begotten of the dead [Priest]
    C) Ruler of the kings of the earth [King]. He is absolutely sovereign and His name is above all names.
4. The Triune God is the Person sending the prophetic message forth to the churches.
5. In looking at the three Persons of the Trinity it should be noted that the book of Revelation is dedicated to Christ alone.

VIII. The Provisions of The Savior (5b-6a)
1. Christ loves unconditionally.
    A) Love is in the present tense in the Greek. This means He always loves us.
    B) Romans 8:37-39 Nothing shall be able to separate us from the love of God.
2. Christ released us from our sins by His blood.
    A) KJV (washed)
    B) NASB (released)
    C) We are set free from sin and death.
    D) The precious blood of Jesus has satisfied the justice of a Holy God.
    E) Ephesians 1:7 "In whom we have redemption through His blood, the forgiveness of sins, according to the riches of His grace." (KJV)
    F) 1 Peter 1:18-19 "Knowing that you were not redeemed with perishable things like silver or gold from your futile way of life inherited from your forefathers, but with precious blood, as of a lamb unblemished and spotless, the blood of Christ."

3. He has made us to be a kingdom of priest.
   A) We have been granted the privilege of divine access to the Father.
   B) 1 Peter 2:9-10
   C) We exercise spiritual authority as we serve God in this world.
   D) Christ has blessed us with power among men and with God.

IX. The Praise To The Savior (6b)

1. There is no doubt because of His mighty deeds on our behalf alone, He is worthy.
2. Jesus laid His glory aside when He came to earth but there is coming a day when all mankind will come to acknowledge Him in all of His glory as the King of kings and Lord of lords.
3. Revelation 5:12

One of the most fascinating and thrilling events discussed in the Bible is the Second Coming of Jesus Christ. The book of Revelation is without a doubt one of the most action packed books in all of the Word of God. One event that makes this true is the Second Coming of Jesus Christ.

The fact that Jesus is coming again gives hope to the Christian and motivation to live a life of purity in light of His coming. In Revelation 1:7, after the introduction John says, "Behold." John is calling the listeners and readers to pay close attention to what is to follow. Therefore, we too must turn our minds and hearts to consider what God has to say regarding the Second Coming.

I. **Why Christ Must Come (7a)**
    1. Scripture demands that Christ return.
        A) Revelation 1:7 "Behold, He is coming…"
        B) Daniel 7:13 "I kept looking in the night visions, And behold, with the clouds of heaven One like a Son of Man was coming, And He came up to the Ancient of Days and was presented before Him."
        C) Jesus promised He would return in John 14:1-3, "Let not your heart be troubled; believe in God, believe also in Me. In My Father's house are many dwelling places; if it were not so, I would have told you. And if I go and prepare a place for you, I will come again, and receive you to myself; that where I am, there you may be also."
        D) Jesus told us that the Holy Spirit would also tell us of things to come. John 16:13 states, "But when He, the Spirit of truth comes, He will guide you into all truth; for He will not speak on His own initiative, but whatever He

hears, He will speak; and He will disclose to you what is to come."

E) One can see from Scripture that the promise of Jesus' return rest on the words of the Trinity.

II. How Christ Will Come (7a)

1. *"...with the clouds..."*
2. This statement is easily understood when one looks through God's Word and recollects the numerous times a cloud was associated with the presence of God.
3. John Phillips said, "The clouds are the clothing of His glory."
4. Many times we find the cloud with God's presence.
   A) Wilderness Wandering
   B) Tent of Meeting
   C) The dedication of the Temple
   D) God's glory departing the Temple in Ezekiel
   E) The Ascension of Jesus in Acts 1:9-11.
5. When Christ returns He will come in all of His glory and splendor and majesty.
6. Remember **Daniel 7:13** spoke of Christ coming with the clouds.

III. Who Will See Christ Come (7b)

1. *"Every eye will see Him, even those who pierced Him..."*
   A) **Zechariah 12:10** "And I will pour out on the house of David and on the inhabitants of Jerusalem, the Spirit of grace and of supplication, so that they will look on Me whom they have pierced; and they will mourn for Him, as one mourns for an only son, and they will weep bitterly over Him like the bitter weeping over a first born."
   B) This speaks of the Jewish nation who rejected Christ and plotted His death.
2. *"And all the tribes of the earth will mourn over Him."*
   A) All the tribes of the earth refers to the Gentiles.

B) **Matthew 24:30** "And then shall appear the sign of the Son of man in heaven: and then shall all the tribes of the earth mourn, and they shall see the Son of man coming in the clouds of heaven with power and great glory."

3. *"The earth will mourn over Him…"*
   A) Some mourn due to the terror of the One who comes to judge.
   B) Some mourn and are penitent.

4. It must be noted that His coming spoken of here in Revelation 1:7 is not the Rapture when Christ comes in the air for His church.

5. The coming spoken of in Revelation 1:7 will be visible to all, and will be the climax at the end of the Tribulation Period.

6. Zechariah 14 tells us He will set His feet on the Mount of Olives and He will be King over all the earth.

IV. The Attributes of The One Who Comes (8)

1. *"The Alpha and the Omega."*
   A) First and last letters of the Greek alphabet.
   B) This speaks of perfect and reliable knowledge.
   C) The One who comes in omniscient.

2. *"Who is and who was and who is to come…"*
   A) The Lord is unchanging and eternal (Heb. 13:8).
   B) The Lord transcends time.
   C) The One who comes is omnipresent.

3. *"The Almighty"*
   A) The Lord is Almighty (pantokrator). He is all Ruler and Controller.
   B) Colossians 1:15-17
   C) Christ has all power.
   D) The One who comes is omnipotent.

Conclusion:

Leaders rise and fall as do nations of the world. However, there is One who comes, mightier and greater than all. Of His kingdom there shall be no end.

Isaiah 9:6-7

<u>**THE GLORIFIED CHRIST**</u>
<u>**REVELATION 1:9-20**</u>

I.   The Victim John Became (9)
1.   John identifies himself as a brother and fellow par-taker (sharing) much tribulation.
2.   John was a victim of intense persecution because of:
     A)   The Word of God
     B)   The Testimony of Jesus.
3.   It was because of John's witness that he was exiled to a rocky, volcanic island called Patmos.
4.   To be a Christian in John's day not only meant persecution but also for many it meant death.
5.   Christianity was considered a criminal activity.
     A)   Merchants who profited from idol worship saw the Christians as an economic threat.
     B)   The Christians were seen as disloyal because they would not acknowledge Caesar as the supreme authority.
     C)   Christians were denounced as atheist.

II.   The Voice John Heard (10-11)
1.   "The Lord's Day" most likely refers to the first day of the week, Sunday.
2.   Here we find John in an attitude of worship as he stated, "I was in the Spirit…"
     A)   He was exiled yet before Christ.
     B)   He was in Christ yet still on earth.
     C)   He was persecuted yet able to praise. (Acts 16, Paul and Silas sang praises at midnight.)
3.   John heard a voice that was loud like the sound of a trumpet.
     A)   **1 Thessalonians 4:16**

B)   This voice is one of authority that John hears.

4.   John was given the command to, "Write in a book what you see." (**v. 11**)

5.   John not only hears what he is to write but where he is to send the message given to him. (**v. 11**)

III. The Vision John Saw (12-16, 20)

1.   As John turned to see the voice he saw seven golden lamp stands or candlesticks.

A)   Golden – precious metal; the church is precious to Jesus.

B)   Seven – completeness

C)   Christ is in the midst of His churches; He indwells His churches.

2.   The description of the One John saw:

A)   "Clothed in a robed and girded across His chest with a golden sash." (**v. 13**)

a)   The dress of a king

b)   The dress of a priest

c)   **Hebrews 4:14-16**

B)   "Hair like white wool and snow." (**v. 14**)

a)   The Ancient of Days (Daniel 7:9)

b)   Purity (white) "Who committed no sin, nor was and deceit found in His mouth." (1 Pt. 2:22).

C)   "Eyes like a flame of fire." (**v. 14**)

a)   He is omniscient and knows all things and sees all things.

b)   "And there is no creature hidden from His sight, but all things are open and laid bare to the eyes of Him with whom we have to do." (Hebrews 4:13)

c)   1 Peter 4:17 tells us that judgment must begin at the house of God.

D)   "Feet like burnished bronze." (brass)

    a)   This speaks of judgment.

    b)   **Revelation 19:15** "…and He treads the wine press of the fierce wrath of God, the Almighty."

    c)   **Genesis 3:15** "And I will put enmity between you and the woman, and between your seed and her seed; He shall bruise you on the head, and you shall bruise Him on the heel."

    d)   There is nothing or no one that can stand in the way of the Victorious Christ.

E)   "The voice like the sound of many waters." (**v. 15**)

    a)   We have the emphasis of power.

    b)   Someone has said to argue with Christ would be like trying to argue with Niagara Falls.

    c)   His is the voice of power and authority.

    d)   The final say will be His alone.

F)   "In His right hand He held seven stars." (**v. 16**)

    a)   "Stars" (**v. 20**) angels or messengers of the seven churches.

    b)   To be in His hand means that He is in control.

    c)   There is nothing that overtakes Christ because He overrules all things.

G)   "Mouth, sharp two-edged sword." (**v. 16**)

    a)   **Hebrews 4:12**

    b)   **Revelation 19:15**

    c)   The Word, His Word has all power.

H)   "His face like the sun shining in its strength." (**v. 16**)

    a)   Radiance, glory, majesty, splendor.

    b)   Imagine trying to approach the sun that is some 93 million miles away. You would be consumed.

    c)   The majesty of His countenance reminds us of His Transfiguration in Mark 9:1-9.

    d)   The Apostle Paul saw Christ in his salvation experience in Acts 9.

IV. The Veneration John Gave (17-18)

1. Upon seeing the vision of the glorified Christ John fell at His feet as a dead man.
2. To encounter Christ results in worship for John and so should it be for the Christian today.
3. The Lord said to John, "Stop being afraid," and gave him reassurance and comfort.
   A) The First and Last (**v. 17**) The Eternal Lord
   B) The Living One…alive forever more (**v. 18**) This is the Resurrected Lord who has conquered death, hell, and the grave.
   C) "I have the keys to death and hades." (**v. 18**)
      a) To have the keys means He has final authority.
      b) **Hebrews 2:14-15**

V. The Verification John Received (19)

1. John again is told to write. (**v. 11**)
   A) "The things which you have seen," (<u>Past</u>) He had seen the Glorified Christ.
   B) "The things which are," (<u>Present</u>) This is the church age, a time of peace.
   C) "The things which will take place after these things," (<u>Future</u>) The deals with the events spoken of in Chapters 4-22.

Conclusion:

The emphasis in Revelation 1:9-20 is the Glorified Christ. As John turned to see the voice speaking, he fell in awe before Christ. Are you in awe of Him?

"What the church needs today is a new awareness of Christ and His glory. We need to see Him "High and lifted up"(Isaiah 6:1). There is a dangerous absence of awe and worship in our assemblies today. We are busy boasting about standing on our own feet, instead of breaking and falling at His feet." (Warren Wiersbe, *The Bible Exposition Commentary*, Vol. 2, page 570)

THE CHURCH THAT WAS SHIFTING AWAY
REVELATION 2:1-7

We now enter the second portion of the book as we recall the outline of the book given in Revelation 1:19.

1. Write about the things which you have seen. (The glory of Christ)
2. The Things that are (church age).
3. The things which shall be after these things.

As John addresses the seven churches of Revelation we must be reminded that these letters are for all churches of all times. Even though John was addressing seven churches of the first century the message is still applicable and is relevant for the churches of today.

When we think of Ephesus one is reminded of Paul's ministry there on his second and third missionary journey as found in Acts 18-20. Most of Paul's ministry was done on the third missionary journey. Scripture tells us that Paul's ministry was not alone. Timothy, Onesiphorus, Tychicus, and the apostle John were pastors at Ephesus. John was most likely at the Ephesian church when he was exiled to Patmos.

Ephesus was a major city in Asia Minor and perhaps the most important of the seven mentioned in Chapters 2-3. The city was well known as the center of worship for the goddess Artemis (Diana to the Romans). Acts 19 reveals that this pagan practice and its economic importance to the merchants in Ephesus was being threatened as many people were coming to faith in Christ. However, there was still much immorality in the city of Ephesus. Not only was the city known for the worship of the pagan goddess, Artemis but was referred to by the geographer, Strabo, as the market of Asia. Ephesus was a primary harbor for Asia.

I. The Description of Christ (1)

1. *"The One who holds the seven stars…"*
   A) **Revelation 1:16, 20**
   B) These stars are the messengers of the churches to which John was writing.
   C) Christ holds them which signifies they are under His control and authority.
2. *"The One who walks…lampstands."*
   A) **Revelation 1:13**
   B) Christ walks among, in the midst of His churches.
   C) Christ sees the inside and with His eyes as a flame of fire (**1:14**). He sees the true condition of the church.

II. The Deeds of The Church (2-3, 6)

1. Toil (kopos)
   A) Labor (KJV) – to the point of exhaustion.
   B) They were dedicated giving all they had.
2. Perseverance (KJV-patience) hupomone
   A) Having patience when the circumstances are difficult and trying. We need this same persistence today and people with commitment.
   B) They were holding up under pressure.
3. They were sensitive to sin (**2**)
   A) They refused to tolerate evil men.
   B) They separated themselves as a holy people.
4. They were spiritually discerning. (**2**)
   A) *"Put to the test those…apostles."*
   B) In 1 John 4:1-6 they were told to try the spirits.
5. *"Perseverance* (patience) *and have endured…"* (**3**)
   A) The church had remained faithful and their motive was for the name of Christ.
   B) In their labor and toil they had not grown weary.

C) **Galatians 6:9** "Let us not lose heart in doing good, for in due time we will reap if we do not grow weary."
6. *"You hate the deeds of the Nicolaitans."*
   A) **Revelation 2:14-15**
   B) Nicolaitanism involved false teaching, eating things sacrificed to idols, and acts of immorality.
   C) Nicolaitan – means to conquer the people. There was an ecclesiastical hierarchy in the church.

III. The Declaration Against The Church (4)
1. *"…you have left your first love."*
2. "And He said to him, 'You shall love the Lord your God with all your heart, and with all your soul, and with all your mind'." (Matthew 22:37)
3. What does it mean to have left your first love?
   A) Passion for Christ has become passive.
   B) Ministry has become mechanical.
   C) Affection had turned into apathy.
   D) They had labor but they lacked love.
   E) They had doctrine but lacked devotion.
4. John Phillips states, "If service for God is not born of a devoted passion for the Lord Jesus it is worth-less."
5. For Ephesus rich love had become routine labor.
6. The next generation at Ephesus was busy maintaining. Devotion had diminished and was drifting away.
   A) This was characteristic of the harbor at Ephesus.
   B) The harbor was continually silting; water became land and land became water.
   C) Just as the harbor had continued to shift so was the case with the church in their love for Christ.

IV. The Direction For The Church (5)
1. <u>Remember</u> the way things used to be.
   A) Conversion to salvation

    B) Call to service
    C) Commitment to the Savior
    D) Communion with the Savior

2. <u>Repent</u> of the way things are.
    A) Repent of doing ministry with the wrong motive.
    B) Repent of performing labor without love.
    C) Repent of serving from a sense of duty rather than one of devotion.
    D) **1 Peter 4:17** Let repentance and judgment begin with the household of God as Christ walks among the church, His church.

3. <u>Recapture</u> the things that should be.
    A) It's about love not labor.
    B) It's about devotion not duty.
    C) It's about worship not work.
    D) It's about passion not programs.
    E) It's about prayer and His presence.

V. The Danger Facing The Church (5)

1. *"...remove your lampstand out of its place..."*
2. When love has shifted and drifted away the fire is gone and with the fire the light is gone.
3. Where there is no love there is no light and that means there is no witness.
4. When love vanishes the reason for the church's existence also vanishes.
5. How many churches have been removed by Christ?
6. Is this church in danger of being removed by Christ?
    A) Has His presence been replaced by a program?
    B) Is His ministry a blessing or a burden?
    C) Has love for Him been replaced by labor?
    D) Is the church lifeless, dull, mechanical, and nothing more than mere form?

VI. The Duty of The Church (7)

1.   There is a personal responsibility to hear the message given.
2.   Your relationship with Christ is personal.
3.   The churches also have a responsibility to hear and obey the message.
4.   The promise is given to the one who overcomes.
     A)   The tree of life (Eternal Life)
     B)   Paradise (Eternal love, joy, peace, fulfillment.

Conclusion:

The distinguishing mark of a Christian is love. Christ said to Ephesus, *"You have fallen."* In 1 Corinthians 13:1 Paul said if we do not have love we are nothing more than a noisy gong and a clanging cymbal. Often John spoke of love in his epistle to the church. When Paul wrote to the Ephesians he prayed they would have more love. Whether it be an individual or whether it be the church corporately, when love is lost, life is gone. When life is gone there is no breath and therefore, there is no witness.

   Have you left your first love? If so, remember how it used to be. Repent of the way things are. Recapture your passion and love for Jesus.

SMYRNA: THE PERSECUTED CHURCH
(THE POOR RICH CHURCH)
REVELATION 2:8-11

Smyrna is associated with the word myrrh. Myrrh was a gum-like resin which was taken from a shrub. It was used for embalming, relieving or dulling pain, and also for perfume. Myrrh was very bitter. It could be said that Smyrna was living out its name. The church was undergoing severe and very bitter persecution.

The city of Smyrna, called the first city of Asia, has a unique history of survival. The city survived numerous earthquakes and fires. It still exists today as the Turkish city of Izmir. Smyrna was identified as being a center of science and medicine. It was said to be the most beautiful city of Asia. This was a city proud of its culture and social life. However, like Ephesus, it was a city of pagan worship and idolatry with temples to Cybele, Zeus, Apollo, Asklepios, and also Aphrodite, not to mention the center of emperor worship as well. When the Christians would not accept the pantheistic culture of their day they were then considered to be atheists and were put out of the social life of the city and also the trade guilds. This led to poverty and great persecution for the Christian in this time.

I. **The Characteristics of Christ (8)**
1. *"The First and the Last..."*
    A) Christ is eternal and the Supreme Authority.
    B) This is an Old Testament title for God.
    C) Being the First and Last He transcends all time.
2. *"Who was dead, and has come to life..."*
    A) This of course speaks of His resurrection. There is a greater message here for the church.
        a) He became dead, meaning it was a passing thing He had to go through.

      b)   He triumphed over death in great victory.

      c)   The word *"alive"* speaks of a once for all act. It is completed, it is finished, alive forever more.

3.   Jesus is telling the church that even though persecu-tion may mean death, it is a passing thing and they will experience victory as He has done.

4.   1 Peter 1:3-4

II. The Commendation To The Church (9)

1.   *Tribulation* (thlipsis) means affliction, the pressure of crushing affliction and persecution.

2.   *Poverty* – possessing absolutely nothing, just surviving.

    A)   Christians were excluded from the trade guilds because they refused to be a part of the emperor worship and to include Christ as one of the many gods to be worshipped. The Christians faced being starved out.

    B)   *"The blasphemy of those who say they are Jews and are not….Satan."*

       a)   These are Jews who rejected Jesus Christ.

       b)   The Jewish synagogue was actually a synagogue of Satan.

       c)   The Jews in Smyrna were persecuting the true followers of Christ. These Jews were very influential in the city among the officials and Roman government. (Polycarp was martyred.)

3.   *But you are rich."*

    A)   The Christians in Smyrna weren't rich materially but were rich spiritually.

    B)   They were rich toward the Lord.

    C)   Philippians 3:8 (Paul)

    D)   Hebrews 11:24-26 (Moses)

III. The Comfort Given To The Church (10)

1. Jesus tells of coming persecution but He will give them strength to endure what is to come.
2. The Lord is aware of what is to come and would allow the Christians to be tested and tried.
3. Results of persecution and trials:
   A) They would be tested; purity and strength would result.
   B) Through persecution spiritual strength would come.
   C) True faith would be a testimony to the world.
   D) John MacArthur stated, "The purest Christian graces are those forged in the furnace of adversity.
4. 2 Corinthians 12:9-10
5. *Ten Days*
   A) Brevity of persecution
   B) Intense and brief (The rack, boiling oil, wild animals, tied to stakes and burned)
   C) Persecution will be limited.

IV. The Crown To Be Received (10)
1. *Crown* (stephanos) this is the victor's crown.
   A) Smyrna was a participant in the annual athletic games.
   B) The Christians would quickly relate the crown to the victory they would experience because they would remain faithful.
   C) The crown of life is synonymous with eternal life.
   D) Man may kill the body but he cannot kill the soul.
2. The message to the church today is still the same, "*Do not fear, be faithful.*"
3. God promises the Christian victory in the journey of faith.

V. The Charge To The Church (11)
1. The believers have the responsibility to hear the message and obey it as well.
2. This message was to Smyrna but it is also a valid message for the church today.

3.   God's promise to those who overcome is that they will not be hurt by the second death.
     A)   Revelation 20:14 describes the second death as the lake of fire.
     B)   This is the judgment of eternal hell and torment.

Conclusion:

Although the church as we know it today faces very little, if any persecution like that of Smyrna, we must be prepared and willing to do so. The day will most likely come when trial and tribulation will confront the church as it takes its stand for Christ in this post modern world. Smyrna is a testimony of what the true church should be. They faithfully confessed Jesus before all men and because of that testimony many were martyred. Hold fast the message and proclaim Christ without shame. persecution, tribulation, and trial may come to you but those who are faithful will be overcomers.

<u>PERGAMUM: THE COMPROMISING CHURCH
REVELATION 2:12-17</u>

The city of Pergamum was located one hundred miles north of Ephesus. Pergamum was a city with a royal air about it. Ephesus was identified as a political center, Smyrna as a commercial center, and Pergamum was identified as the religious center of its day. Pergamum was known for it massive library of some 200,000 volumes, second only to Alexandria in Egypt. The city was built atop a mountain approximately 1000 feet high. Pergamum is symbolic of churches from about 312 A.D. to 600 A.D.

I. **The Characteristics of Christ (12)**
    1. Christ is identified as the One having the sharp two edged sword.
    2. Revelation 1:16 (John's vision of Christ)
    3. This is the only church where Christ identifies Him-self twice **(2:12; 2:16)**.
    4. This identification speaks of the Word of God.
        A) Hebrews 4:12
        B) Ephesians 6:17
    5. His Word is power and authority.

II. **The Commendation To The Church (13)**
    1. The church is commended for their place and their presence in the city. This was a great metropolitan area.
        A) They were dwelling in a place with difficulties and trying circumstances.
        B) They had been placed there to make a difference as churches are to do today.
    2. Christ said Pergamum was where "*Satan's throne is….*"
        A) Pergamum was a city known for idolatrous worship.
            a) Altar of Zeus – 90 feet square and 40 feet high

      b)   Athena – god of drama and god of art

      c)   Asklepios – god of healing (serpent) Many would spend the night in the temples believing that one of the non-poisonous serpents might touch them and thereby bring healing.

      d)   Dionysius – (Bacchus) god of wine; goat god

      e)   Pergamum was the first city to have a temple dedicated to Caesar. Emperor worship was compulsory.

   B)   Antipas would not yield and lost his life.

      a)   **Revelation 1:5** Christ was the faithful witness (martyr).

      b)   Christ called Antipas, "My faithful one."

      c)   Antipas identified with Christ. There was dedication without denial.

      d)   **John 16:2; Philippians 1:29**

3.   The Christians at Pergamum are commended.

   A)   They held fast Jesus' name (deity).

   B)   They had not denied the faith (doctrine).

   C)   They had endured great pressure with no compromise

4.   There is no amount of Satanic opposition that can destroy genuine saving faith.

5.   It was better for them to fear the sword of Christ than to fear the sword of Rome.

III. The Complaint To The Church (14-15)

1.   The church was compromising.

2.   To compromise is to surrender one's principles to a lower nature or cause.

3.   A church, denomination, or an individual must not compromise.

   A)   Society says, "Be tolerant." Some Christians are also afraid that they will offend someone.

B) You may be accused of being narrow minded and unloving.

C) False doctrine and a willingness to compromise is wrong. God's Word is truth!

4. When an individual dilutes his life he cannot be an effective witness and loses his testimony.

5. Christ's complaint was twofold:

A) *Teaching of Balaam* (lord of the people).

    a) Balak the Moabite king hired Balaam to curse Israel. (Numbers 22-25)

    b) When Balaam could not curse Israel he told Balak to corrupt them. This was done by inter-marriage with the Moabite women.

    c) God judged Israel and 24,000 people died.

    d) Fornication and idolatrous worship resulted as Israel made friends with the enemy.

    e) The true Christians of Pergamum were cut off from the social life of the city.

B) *Teaching of the Nicolaitans* (conquer the laity)

    a) John Phillip's - "Let's be more restricted in our leadership."

    b) They wanted to build an ecclesiastical body.

    c) In 312 A.D. Constantine, a Roman general pulled off one of the greatest political moves ever made. It is said that he saw a flaming cross in the sky and heard a voice which said, "By this sign conquer." It was then that the Christian church was married to Rome and paganism.

    d) Pergamum means "married". This should be a reminder to the Christian that the church is engaged to Jesus Christ.

    e) Men tried to take the Scriptures out of the hands of the ecclesiastical body and they lost their lives for

their actions. (Dark Ages)
6. There is a short step from compromising with the world to forsaking Christ altogether.

IV. The Challenge To The Church (16-17)
1. Repent (metanieo)
   A) To repent is to have a change of mind.
   B) The change of mind results in a change of behavior.
2. God will war against or fight against those who do not repent.
   A) He is able to discern between the wheat and chaff.
   B) He is able to discern between the sheep and the goats.
3. Unless repentance comes God will withdraw His presence and power.
   A) No Holy Spirit – no power, spiritual impotence
   B) No love – no light and no witness
   C) No mission – no giving
   D) Empty prayer meetings, empty singing, disunity, disharmony, confusion, no growth.
4. Blessings and growth come when Christ has His rightful place in the hearts of His people.
5. Christ's promise:
   A) *Hidden Manna*
      a) John 6:35 refers to Jesus as the Bread of Life.
      b) Spiritual food and understanding
      c) Nourishment and satisfaction
   B) *White Stone*
      a) A piece of ivory in a cube or rectangular was given to intimate friends (tessera). It would have words or symbols engraved on it.
      b) The stone could also mean forgiveness.
      c) Athletic victors were given a white stone and this were their ticket to a special awards banquet.

C) *New Name*
- a) The intimate Lord will give the believer a name of Himself no one else can share.
- b) His name and identity speak of a relationship to His own.

Conclusion:

One theologian said that the user friendly, seeker oriented, market driven church doesn't preach much against worldliness. It is poor marketing strategy. A church that doesn't confront worldliness and the reality of sin is repeating the same mistake made by the church at Pergamum. Judgment faces that church. To tolerate worldliness, false doctrine and sin is to compromise and thereby share in the guilt of those sins.

Individuals say you can't live in this age and be a separated Christian. If you don't live a separated life you can lose your testimony and your witness and thereby you end up denying Christ.

(Romans 12:2; James 1:27; 1 John 2:15-17)

<u>THYATIRA: THE PERMISSIVE CHURCH
REVELATION 2:18-29</u>

It is not definite how the church at Thyatira began. There has been raised often the possibility that Lydia and those of her household were instrumental in the launching of the church at Thyatira (Acts 16:14). Another view is that the church at Thyatira was an overflow from Paul's ministry at Ephesus as found in Acts 19. At the time the apostle John wrote this letter the church would have been approximately forty years old and experiencing a time of prosperity. At this time Thyatira was not a religious center like Pergamos but was more of a commercial center with an industry of wool and goods dyed with purple. There were many trade guilds and each one of them had their own pagan deity who was honored at certain feasts. The livelihood of Christians was threatened if they did not attend these feasts and honor the pagan deities. The prominent god that was worshipped in Thyatira was Apollo, the sun god of the Greeks. Thyatira was also a military garrison and an outpost for the city of Pergamos. It was destroyed and rebuilt many times because it lacked the resources of fortification. It was a city located in a valley southeast of the city of Pergamos.

I.   **The Attributes of Christ (18)**
1.   John writes to Thyatira the longest of the letters to the seven churches and it is the smallest city.
2.   In addressing Thyatira John again gives us the attributes of Christ. These focus on divine judgment.
     A) *"The Son of God"* – This is the only time that this description is given in the book of Revelation. It is important remember that Thyatira worshipped Apollo, the sun god of the Greeks.

B) *"Eyes like a flame of fire"* – Nothing can be hidden from the penetrating vision of Christ. (2:23)

C) *"His feet are like burnished bronze"* – This speaks of the judgment that the church would experience because of the seriousness of its sin and unrepentant spirit by some.

II. The Affirmation of Christ (19)

1. Christ assesses and emphasizes the deeds or work of the church.
2. The believers are commended for their love for God and for others.
3. Thyatira is commended also for their faith.
   A) Faith (pistis)
   B) Fidelity; Faithfulness
   C) The believers could be relied upon and were very dependable
4. The church is also commended for its service and perseverance (patience).
   A) The love they possessed was expressed in service.
   B) The faith they possessed was seen in how they persevered with great endurance.
5. Jesus said, "Your deeds of late are greater than at first."
   A) They were growing in their love, faith, service, and perseverance.
   B) They were maturing and growing in Christ.

III. The Accusation of Christ (20)

1. The church was tolerating one identified as Jezebel (probably a symbolic name due to wickedness).
   A) The church was being permissive.
   B) This woman had assumed leadership in the church (I Timothy 2:12-14) which contradicts the Word.

    C) This so called prophetess was allowed to teach error and lead people astray (**2:24**).

    D) People were involved in acts of immorality and eating things sacrificed to idols.

2. This false teacher no doubt had many of the same characteristics as her counterpart of the Old Testament.

    A) **1 Kings 16-19**

    B) Influenced Israel in Baal worship.

    C) Ahab's wife, Jezebel was the most wicked woman in all of the Old Testament.

3. Believers were compromising with pagan religion and the trade guilds to keep their jobs and possibly avoid death.

4. Idolatry and compromise is spiritual adultery.

5. Christ looks for a church where there is purity and holiness.

IV. The Approach of Christ (21)

1. A time of grace was extended that repentance might come.

2. This offer of grace was rejected and refused.

3. The longsuffering and patience of the Lord was met with stubbornness and a desire to continue in sin.

4. 2 Peter 3:9 states God is not willing for any to perish but for all to come to repentance.

V. The Action of Christ (22-23)

1. In these verses the Lord says three times, "*I will...*"as He speaks of His intent to judge.

2. Judgment is threefold:

    A) "*I will throw her on a bed of sickness...* (Jezebel)

    B) "*Those who commit adultery with her...*"

        a) Great tribulation may refer to a time of trouble and chastisement.

        b) Physical death may occur (**1 John 5:16**).

    C) "*I will kill her children with pestilence.*"

        a) The followers of this "Jezebel" were her children.

b) Pestilence refers to death.
3. Christ will purify His church.
   A) Acts 5 : Ananias and Sapphira lied and died.
   B) 1 Corinthians 11:30
4. The One with the eyes as a flame of fire searches the minds and hearts. He knows those who belong to Him and He knows the hearts of all men.

VI. The Admonition of Christ (24-25)

1. The Lord comforts and encourages those who have stood true and faithful.
   A) They had not followed Jezebel's teaching.
   B) They had not known the deep things of Satan.
2. The Lord would place no other burden on them.
   A) They had not followed the crowd.
   B) They had been strong in rejecting false doctrine.
   C) They had been burdened by immorality.
3. They are told to hold fast until come.
   A) *Hold Fast* (krateo) – This would be a most difficult task for the believers.
   B) The believers would face ridicule and rejection but must remain devoted to Christ.

VII. The Awards of Christ (26-29)

1. To the overcomer who is steadfast in his obedience:
   A) He will reign with Christ.
      a) Millennial Reign
      b) Psalm 2:7-9
   B) He will receive the Morning Star.
      a) This is Jesus Christ Himself.
      b) When one has Christ they have everything.

Conclusion:

Smyrna – The Synagogue of Satan

Pergamos – The Seat or throne of Satan
Thyatira – The deep things of Satan

Ephesus was sound in doctrine and lacking in love and devotion. Thyatira was sound in love and lacking in doctrine and purity. In the second century this church was out of existence. A church cannot tolerate evil and be permissive and expect to remain. When a church departs from sound doctrine and the Word of God it is on its way to breathing its final breath.

SARDIS: LIVING ON PAST GLORY
REVELATION 3:1-6

Astronomers tell us that the nearest stars to us are trillions of miles away. These distances are measured in what is called light years. For instance, one light year equals the distance that light, traveling at more than 186,000 miles per second travels in one year. This would be more than six (6) trillion miles. If you think of the nearest star to us being thirty (30) light years and that star exploding and dying five years ago, we would not be able to tell by looking at it for twenty five years. Even though that star was no longer in existence, the light would go on shining as if nothing had happened.

Sardis was the capital of the kingdom of Lydia in Asia Minor. It was one of the oldest and most important cities in Asia Minor. Sardis was located about fifty miles east of Ephesus and about thirty miles south of Thyatira. The city of Sardis was situated atop a plateau approximately 1500 feet high. This made it virtually impossible for the city to be overtaken by an enemy. Sardis for that reason was a mil- itary fortress but also a center for trade. It was in a prime location where several main roads came together. Being a commercial center, Sardis produced wool garments. Sardis worshipped Artemis (Diana) which was their main religion. The church at Sardis was like the exploding star, shining solely on the light of a bright history and former glory.

I. **The Ruling Christ (1)**
    1. "*Seven Spirits*" speaks of the fullness and completeness of the Holy Spirit (**1:4**).
        A) It was through the Holy Spirit that we see the birth of the church in Acts 2 at Pentecost.
        B) It is the Spirit that gives life.

2. *"Seven Stars"* are the messengers of the churches in the hands of the Ruling Christ (**1:16**).

3. It is Christ who is the Head and center of the church.

II. The Reproach of The Church (1)

1. The church has a name that they are alive but Christ said they were dead.

2. Sardis was a church populated with the unredeemed who were playing church.

3. This church was like Jesus' parable of the figtree, there were leaves but no fruit.

4. What is interesting is what Jesus did not say.
   A) There is no mention of immorality.
   B) There is no mention of persecution.
   C) There is no mention of false teachers.
   D) There is no mention of false doctrine.

5. Sardis was a church going through the motions yet it was devoid of the Spirit of God.

6. Sardis may have been like many churches today with every program possible, busy yet dead.

7. The danger signs of death:
   A) When a church lives on past glory.
   B) When a church is more concerned with form and tradition rather than spiritual reality.
   C) When a church is more concerned with healing the social ills rather than healing the hearts of men with the proclamation of the Gospel message.
   D) When the church becomes more concerned with material things rather than spiritual things.
   E) When the church becomes more concerned about what man says and thinks rather than what God's Word says.

8. Vance Havner said spiritual ministries usually go through four stages: a man, a movement, a machine, and finally a

monument.

9. The church at Sardis had become like the city; it had become comfortable, complacent, content, and over confident.

10. The city had changed the church rather than the church changing it surroundings.

III. The Remaining Work (2)
1. Their work was not complete according to Christ.
2. They were to strengthen the spiritual things that remain.
3. They were to wake up and fan the dying flames.
4. Sardis perhaps was good at starting something and not finishing or completing it.
5. It is not certain what things remained but they were in danger of being lost.

IV. The Requirements or Responsibility of The Church (3)
1. Remember
   A) What you have received: The Word of God
   B) What you have heard: The Word of God
   C) Keep it: The Word of God – Doctrinal Purity
   D) The authority of the Word of God is critical to the life of any church. Depart from the Word and death is imminent.
2. Repent
   A) Complacency
   B) Let this be a time of self examination.
   C) Return to the way things should be.
3. Recognize the time.
   A) Wake up and watch.
      a) Sardis was twice captured and overthrown.
      b) Medes and Persians – 549 B.C.
      c) Antiochus the Great – 218 B.C.
      d) Sentries were asleep and the city unguarded.

B) Christ would come like a thief.
   a) Unexpected – Just like their enemies had done.
   b) Jesus would come in judgment.
   c) "Looking for the blessed hope and the appearing of the glory of our great God and Savior, Christ Jesus" (Titus 2:13**).**

V. The Remnant of The Church (4)
1. The future of the ministry was in the hands of a remnant.
2. God always has His faithful few.
   A) They had not soiled their garments.
      a) Soiled means to defile, to smear, to pollute.
      b) They had remained faithful and were worthy.
   B) Sardis would understand when Christ spoke about garments since the city was a producer of woolen garments.

VI. The Rewards For The Faithful (5-6)
1. White Garments
   A) Garments were worn on festive occasions such as weddings.
   B) Garments were worn to celebrate victory in battle.
   C) White – symbolic of holiness and purity.
2. Salvation that is secure:
   A) "I will not erase his name…"
   B) "I will confess his name…"
   C) Matthew 10:32

Conclusion:

There is hope for a dying church. There is a pathway to renewal and revival when there is repentance. The warning is clear to those who are comfortable, complacent, content, and self confident. Christ in essence said, "Wake up and look out! I will come unexpectantly in judgment. The church and individual Christians are not to simply to find themselves going through the motions. A Christian is not to live on past victories and former glory days. There is still work to do. Will you be faithful?

PHILADELPHIA: THE FAITHFUL EXAMPLE
REVELATION 3:7-13

Philadelphia was the youngest of the seven cities to which John addresses the letters to the churches. The city was perhaps founded by Attalus II approximately around 189 B.C. He had a nickname which was "Philadelphus" which means "brother lover." Attalus was very loyal to his brother who was named Eumenes, who was king of Pergamum prior to his becoming king. Philadelphia was unlike the other cities in that it was not a military outpost but more of a center of Greek culture. In fact, Philadelphia could have been called a missionary city that spread the Greek culture and along with the Greek language. It was very successful at its task. The city was situated along several trade routes and was called the "gateway to the east." It was also in a volcanic region which earned it the name "burned land." The city was also prone to many earthquakes. It was destroyed by an earthquake in 17 B.C.

The church at Philadelphia has been given many names in which to describe it:

The Missionary Church
The Faithful Church
The Few But Faithful
The Weak But Wonderful Church
The Weak But Willing Church
A Small Church With Spiritual Power
The Little But Loyal Church

I. **The Character of Christ (7)**
    1. He is holy.
        A) Jesus in essence declares He is God.
        B) "Holy, Holy, Holy, is the Lord of hosts, the whole earth is full of His glory." (Isaiah 6:3)

    C) He was holy in His birth (Luke 1:35).
    D) He was holy in His death (Acts 2:27).
    E) He is holy in His priestly office (Heb. 7:26-27).
    F) He will be holy in His coming again (Rev. 19:11f)
2. He is true.
    A) "Jesus said to him, 'I am the way, the truth, and the life; no one comes to the Father but through Me'." (John 14:6)
    B) True (alethinos) means genuine, authentic, or real.

II. The Control of Christ (7)

1. The key of David.
    A) "Key" is symbolic of authority.
    B) "David" speaks of His messianic office.
    C) Eliakim was a steward or an administrator of the affairs of God's people with access to the treasures of the king. (Isaiah 22:22)
    D) Jesus holds the keys to salvation and blessing, regarding the kingdom.
2. "Who opens and no one shuts…"
    A) Christ is all powerful and His regal claims are seen in these words.
    B) It is Christ alone who can open and close which demonstrates His sovereign control and authority.
    C) The saints and the church are under His control, not that of men. He is why we are here!!

III. The Commendation To The Church (8, 10a)

1. Strength – "A little power"
    A) Power – dunamin (dynamite)
    B) Philadelphia most likely did not have impressive numbers, buildings, or budgets like churches of today. Our weakness forces us to depend on Him.
    C) Size does not determine service.

2. Obedience – "Have kept My word"
   A) Philadelphia believed God's word and was faithful to it. Honoring God's Word brings blessings.
   B) "I have not departed from the command of His lips; I have treasured the words of His mouth more than my necessary food." (Job 23:12)
   C) "Your word is a lamp to my feet and a light to my path." (Psalm 119:105)
   D) "Thy word I have treasured in my heart....against You." (Psalm 119:11)
3. Loyalty – "Have not denied My name"
   A) This church was not only a Bible believing church but one that was loyal to the Person of Christ.
   B) Today in some seminaries and pulpits the deity of Christ is questioned regarding the virgin birth, His vicarious death, His victorious resurrection, and His visible coming again.
   C) Let us recall why John was exiled to Patmos (Revelation 1:9).
      a) The Word of God
      b) The testimony of Jesus
4. "You have kept the word of My Perseverance." (10a)
   A) Patience – Endurance
   B) Through trials, persecution, and all the difficulties Philadelphia had been steadfast.
   C) "Be faithful unto death...life." (Revelation 2:10)
   D) Faith in Christ and His word enables one to endure with great patience.

IV. The Challenge/Call of Christ (8, 11, 13)
1. "An open door..." (8)
   A) Opportunity for service and ministry.
   B) Freedom to proclaim the Gospel.

      C)   Faithfulness will result in open doors.
2.   "Hold fast what you have..." (11)
      A)   They had been obedient, loyal, and faithful.
      B)   The church was to remain obedient, loyal, and faithful. They are to watch and work.
      C)   "Crown" – reward for those who remain faithful.
3.   "He who has an ear...churches." (13)
      A)   Hear and heed the message.
      B)   This is a divine invitation to hear and understand.
      C)   A church must see the opportunities before them!

V.   Christ's Comfort For The Church (9-12)

1.   "<u>I will</u> make them come and bow..." **(9)**
      A)   The enemies of the church will bow.
      B)   If we take care to be faithful, He will take care to be faithful regarding the battles and opposition we face.
      C)   Synagogue of Satan – ungodly, unbelieving, Jews in the flesh opposing the church.
2.   "<u>I will</u> keep you from the hour of testing..." (10)
      A)   "From" – out of
      B)   Hour of testing
          a)   The Tribulation Period
          b)   Daniel 9:25-27
          c)   Revelation 6-19
      C)   The church is raptured before the Tribulation.
          a)   John 14:1-4
          b)   1 Corinthians 15:51-54
          c)   1 Thessalonians 4:13-17
3.   "<u>I am</u> coming quickly..." (11)
      A)   Titus 2:13
      B)   His Second Coming will be a time for judgment.
      C)   Here He speaks of coming for His church.
4.   "<u>I will</u> make him a pillar..."(12)

    A) Stability, permanence.
        a) In the city there were pillars inscribed with the names of those who were honored.
        b) Remember also that Philadelphia was a place of many earthquakes. (ref. 17 B.C.)
    B) Pillars were also inscribed in Philadelphia to other deities.
    C) God will honor those who belong to Him.
5. "I will write on Him the name of…"
    A) My God
        a) Relationship
        b) Fellowship
        c) Ownership
    B) City of My God
        a) Citizenship
        b) Security and safety

Conclusion:

"Eye hath not seen, nor ear heard, neither hath entered into the heart of man the things which God hath prepared for them that love Him. (1 Corinthians 2:9)

Philadelphia was faithful in the proclaiming of the Word of God. History tells us that this church lasted until the 13th century. At that time it was destroyed by the Seljuk Turks. They came in and killed all the believers who were left in this church. It is believed that the reason for the Gospel and Christianity moving into India was because of the church at Philadelphia. God placed before them an open door and they seized the opportunity. Will we do the same?

<u>LAODECIA: THE CHURCH REDUCED TO ROOM</u>
<u>TEMPERATURE</u>
<u>REVELATION 3:14-22</u>

Laodecia was founded by Antiochus II, the Seleucid. This was a wealthy and prosperous city. In fact, after an earthquake in A.D. 60, the city paid for its own reconstruction, taking nothing from Rome. Laodecia was one hundred miles east of Ephesus and was the southeastern most of the seven cities spoken of in Revelation. Laodecia was approximately forty miles from Philadelphia.

There are several unique characteristics concerning the city of Laodecia. This city was a banking center, a commercial center which produced soft black wool, and was also an ancient center of medicine. An eye salve was produced in the city.

The church at Laodecia was likely established during Paul's ministry at Ephesus. Epaphras had founded the church at Colossae so he may have founded the church at Laodecia. The church appears to have taken on the characteristics of the city. It is the last church addressed and the worst of all of those mentioned in Revelation. There is no positive word of commendation as God had nothing good to say at all in regards to this church. In fact, this letter is the most threatening letter of all. There are many parallels of the history of Israel and the church at Laodecia. The church was lethargic, self-satisfied, complacent, half-hearted, and characterized by Christ as being "lukewarm."

Lukewarm – "The Rights of the People"

I.   The Characteristics of Christ (14)
    1.   The letter is addressed to the messenger of the church.
        A)   The ultimate responsibility of the church falls on the pastor.

    B)   Often the spiritual temperature of a church is determined by the pastor.

2.   "Amen" (verily, truly)
    A)   This is used as an Old Testament title for God.
    B)   This word declares and affirms the truthfulness of a statement.
    C)   This is a guarantee of the truth.
    D)   Jesus confirms all of God's promises.

3.   "Faithful and True Witness"
    A)   He is reliable, trustworthy, accurate,
    B)   Christ speaks truthfully about the condition of the church.

4.   "Beginning (arche) of the Creation"
    A)   He is the origin or the source of all things.
    B)   The heresy of gnosticism may have been taught at Laodecia which said that Christ was a created being. This would call into question the deity of Christ and His virgin birth, the incarnation.
    C)   When a church strays from who Christ truly is and questions His deity it is destined for destruction.

II.   The Condition of The Church (15-17)

1.   The church was unregenerate, not hot or cold.
    A)   Hot -- would represent a church alive.
    B)   Cold -- would be symbolic of no life at all.
    C)   This church was dead and cold, being insensitive to the sting of sin.

2.   Laodecia was a church that made the Lord sick.
    A)   Lukewarm
        a)   This was a half committed church.(John R.W. Stott) "Perhaps none of the seven letters is more appropriate to the twentieth century church than this. It describes vividly the respectable,

sentimental, nominal, skin-deep religiosity which is so widespread among us today. Our Christianity is flabby and anaemic. We appear to have taken a lukewarm bath in religion. (*What Christ Thinks of the Church* [Grand Rapids: Eerdmans, 1980], 116)
   b) Deeds confirm and give evidence of the presense of genuine salvation.
- B) "…holding to a form of godliness, although they have denied its power; Avoid such men as these." (2 Timothy 3:5)
3. You are lukewarm…" (16)
   A) Colossae was known for its cold pure water.
   B) Heirapolos was known for its hot springs.
   C) There was an aqueduct underground that brought the water into the city. When the cold water along with the water from the hot springs came together in Laodecia it was lukewarm, dirty, and useless.
4. They were self deceived and had a false sense of security. (17)
   A) They said, "I am rich….nothing." "Thomas Aquinas once called upon Pope Innocent II. The pope was counting a large sum of money. 'You see Thomas,' said the pope, 'the church can no longer say, 'Silver and gold have I none.' 'True, holy Father,' said Thomas. 'and neither can it say to the lame any more, 'Arise and walk.'" (*Exploring Revelation* [Neptune: Loizeaux, 1991], p. 74, (John Phillips)
   B) "You are wretched" (hotolaiporos) They were afflicted spiritually.
   C) "Miserable" (eleenios) They were to be pitied and were despicable.
   D) "Poor" (ptochos) They were spiritual paupers.

E) "Blind" (tophlos) They could only see what the world would see.

F) "Naked" (gumnos) They need to be clothed in the righteousness of Christ.

G) "inasmuch as we, having put it on, will not be found naked." 2 Corinthians 5:3

III. The Command of Christ (18)
1. Spiritual Riches -- "Buy from Me gold refined by fire."
   A) Laodecia was a banking center.
   B) They are told to pay the price for true riches.
   C) Philippians 3:8
   D) 1 Peter 1:7
2. Spiritual Raiment -- "White garments"
   A) Laodecia produced soft <u>black</u> wool.
   B) White garments would be symbolic of the righteousness of Christ.
   C) 2 Corinthians 5:17; 5:21
3. Spiritual Revelation -- "Eye salve"
   A) Laodecia was a medical center that produced an eye salve.
   B) John 8:12; 2 Corinthians 4:4

IV. The Compassion of Christ (19-20)
1. "Therefore be zealous and repent."
   A) Repent
   B) Correct behavior and change lives.
2. "Zealous"
   A) Boil
   B) Burn with zeal
   C) Sincerity
3. "Those the Lord loves He disciplines and reproves."
   A) These were evidently unregenerate for the word the Lord uses for love is not the word He uses to speak to

His children. It is phileo not agape.
  B) Hebrews 12:5-6
 4. Christ's compassion is seen also in verse 20.
  A) He is the patient Christ (standing).
  B) He is the pursuing Christ (knocking).
  C) He is the pleading Christ (voice).
  D) He is the promising Christ ("I will come in…")
 5. "Dine" (deipneo)
  A) The evening meal.
  B) The last meal of the day.
  C) Jesus desires to have communion and fellowship.

V. The Commitment of Christ (21-22)
 1. The overcomer will sit with Christ on His throne.
 2. The overcomer will rule and reign with Christ.
 3. "His master said to him, 'Well done, good and faithful slave. You were faithful with a few things, I will put you in charge of many things; enter into the joy of your master'." (Matthew 25:21)

Conclusion:

There are some churches that make the Lord happy. There are some churches that make the Lord angry. But can you imagine a church that would make the Lord sick? Laodecia was such a church. This is a church that represents the time before the Lord will return. Often it has been said that we today live in the Laodecian Age. God help us not to be a church that is half-hearted, half-committed, lethargic, and complacent, self-deceived and self-satisfied. Even with a church like Laodecia Christ's compassion is seen in that he desires to have fellowship and communion with even those where no life is evident. He is a gracious Lord, willing to dine with each of us. As if it were supper time, that time for the last meal of the day, may we spend this time in sweet fellowship and communion with Jesus.

"O, COME LET US ADORE HIM
REVELATION 4

There are many people today who speak of some fascinating vision they have had. It may have been a dream or a so called near death experience. These claims are made almost everyday regarding some kind of religious experience. To believe such claims is not wise. Scripture tells us of at least four (4) individuals who saw heaven in a vision. We recall Daniel spoke of heaven and the Ancient of Days and His seat in heaven. Ezekiel in his call vision describes in Ezekiel 1 the details of what he saw. The apostle Paul in 2 Corinthians 12:4 was caught up into paradise and heard things as he said were, "inexpressible words, which a man is not permitted to speak." Here in Revelation 4 we have the beloved disciple, John and his description of heaven and the throne which he saw. It goes without saying as one reads Revelation 4 that the theme is the throne and heaven is a place of worship. In fact Revelation 4 deals with worship concerning the Creator while Revelation 5 deals with worship concerning the Redeemer.

As we recall Revelation 1:19, God has given us an out line of the book of the Revelation. John was told to write about the things which he had seen, the things which are, and finally the things which will take place after these things. Revelation 4:1 lets us know we are in the third division of Revelation. This will include Chapters 4-22. The scene now shifts from the church age on earth to heaven. John saw an open door and heard a voice like a trumpet speaking to him saying, "Come up here." John is an example to us as to what will happen when the church age comes to a close. This is a sure statement regarding the Rapture of the church (1 Corinthians 15:51-52, 1 Thessalonians 4:13-18) to meet the Lord in the air. John will now view what will take place on earth during the Tribulation Period. First, John will view the throne and the worship of the Lord.

I. The Lord On The Throne (2-3a)
   1. God the Father is on His throne. (2)
      A) God's throne was already there upon John's arrival.
      B) God's throne represents sovereignty.
      C) God's throne represents control and authority.
      D) "Throne was standing" – permanent, unshakable.
   2. God is "sitting" on His throne. (2)
      A) His throne is occupied.
      B) He is reigning and ruling from heaven.
      C) Daniel 7:9-10
   3. The description of God on the throne (3a)
      A) Jasper Stone
         a) Crystal clear – some identify this as a diamond.
         b) The last stone in the breastplate of the high priest.
         c) The jasper stone represented Benjamin, the last born. Benjamin means "the son of my right hand."
      B) Sardius Stone
         a) Fiery red – symbolic perhaps of holiness and justice.
         b) This was first stone in the breastplate of the high priest.
         c) The sardius stone represented Reuben, the first-born. Reuben means "behold, a son."
      C) These stones may be speaking of Christ, the Son who is seated at the Father's right hand.

II. The Rainbow, Elders, And Living Creatures Around The Throne (3b-4; 6-7)
   1. The Rainbow (iris) (3b)
      A) Emerald – The stone is green in appearance and in a complete circle speaking of perfection.
      B) This is a reminder of God's covenant promise.

C) Even in the judgment to come there would be mercy and grace.

2. Twenty Four Elders (presbuteros) (4)
   A) Twenty Four Thrones
      a) They reign with Christ being seated on thrones.
      b) They most likely represent the raptured church.
      c) White Garments speak of purity.
      d) Golden Crown (stephanos) – the victor's crown
      e) These are those who have overcome.
   B) Some suggest this is symbolic of believers of all times: twelve tribes of Israel, twelve apostles, thus showing the completion of God's redeemed.

3. Four Living Creatures (zao) (6-8)
   A) These are in the inner circle around the throne.
   B) These creatures are best understood to be angelic beings.
   C) Full of eyes – wisdom, alertness, insight, aware
   D) Fourfold Description
      a) Lion – Matthew portrays Christ as a King.
      b) Calf – Mark portrays Christ as a servant.
      c) Man – Luke portrays Christ in His humanity.
      d) Eagle – John portrays Christ in His deity.
      e) These creatures remind us of the cherubim in the call vision Ezekiel had. We are also reminded of the cherubim over the mercy seat. The prophet Isaiah spoke of the seraphim with six wings.

III. Signs And Sounds From The Throne (5a)

1. These signs and sounds are indication of a coming storm.
2. This speaks of God's judgment during the Tribulation Period.
   A) Revelation 8:5
   B) Revelation 11:19
   C) Revelation 16:18

3.   God's judgment is indeed something to be feared.

4.   Revelation 6-19 speaks of God's judgment and wrath.

IV. Seven Spirits And The Sea of Glass Before The Throne (5b-6a)

1.   John identifies the seven lamps as representing the seven Spirits of God.

    A)   This speaks of the Holy Spirit in His fullness.

    B)   The work of the Holy Spirit is to reprove the world of sin, righteousness, and judgment. (John 16:18)

2.   Sea of Glass

    A)   God's judgment will be as transparent as crystal.

    B)   The crystal sea is symbolic of His holiness.

    C)   At this judgment there will be no appeals made to the court.

    D)   Unlike the raging waters of the sea this sea of glass changes not.

V. The Worship Towards The Throne (8-11)

1.   He is worshipped because of His holiness. (8)

2.   He is worshipped because of His strength. (8)

3.   He is worshipped because of His eternality. (8)

4.   He is worshipped as Creator.

5.   The elders cast their crowns before the Lord.

    A)   They abandon their own rights giving up their crowns.

    B)   He alone is worthy (axios) of all glory, honor, and power.

6.   Throughout Revelation the elders prostrate themselves before God.

7.   It is the natural response to the Lord as He is seen in all of His glory and majesty. This should be the natural response of every born again believer.

WORTHY IS THE LAMB

REVELATION 5

There should be no break between Chapter 4 and 5. This is a continuous time of praise. Chapter 4 speaks of worship to the Creator and Chapter 5 speaks of the worship given to the Redeemer. Remember, the church is now in heaven and not a part of the Tribulation Period that is taking place on the earth. Heaven is going to be a place of ongoing worship and praise. If you don't like to sing you had better get into practice because heaven is where the redeemed sing.

I. **The Proclamation of The Strong Angel (1-4) "Who is worthy...'**
1. The sealed book.
    A) The title deed to the earth.
    B) All of the earth was searched, all of heaven was searched and no one was found worthy to take the book from the Father's hand.
    C) This book when it is opened will show the judgments that will take place on the earth.
2. The strong angel. ("Who is worthy")
3. The sobbing prophet.

II. **The Presentation of The Standing Lamb (5b-7)**
1. The standing Lamb. (Resurrected)
2. The slain Lamb. (Crucifixion)
3. The strong Lamb. (7 horns) Omnipotent
4. The seeing Lamb. (7 eyes) Omniscient
5. The lamb throughout Scripture:
    A) Genesis 22 – Individual
    B) Exodus 12 – Family

        C)   Isaiah 53 – Nation
        D)   John 1 – World
6.   Lamb – "little baby lamb" – John uses the term "lamb" 28x's in the Revelation.
7.   The Lamb is worthy to take the book because of:
        A)   Creation – He is the Creator of the universe.
        B)   Calvary – He died for the world.
        C)   Conquered – He arose victorious and will reign.

III. The Praise of The Singing Saints (8-14)

1.   Chapter 4 is the worship of the Creator.
2.   Chapter 5 is the worship of the Redeemer.
3.   Someone has said this song includes:
        A)   A worship hymn – "worthy"
        B)   A gospel song – "slain"
        C)   A missionary song – "every kindred, tongue...'
        D)   A devotional song – "priest..."
        E)   A prophetic hymn – "reign"
4.   Jesus came unto His own and they received Him not.
5.   Jesus went to the cross to redeem all of mankind.
6.   Jesus is the Lamb worthy to be praised and adored.

Conclusion:

The decision is man's to receive Christ. However, there will come a day when it will not be man's decision to acknowledge Him as Lord (Philippians 2:9-11).

<u>THE RIDERS OF THE APOCALYPSE</u>
<u>REVELATION 6:1-8</u>

It has been as though one has been listening to a concert in heaven. Revelation 4 and 5 are given to worship and praise of the Creator and the Redeemer respectively. Those who are involved in worship are singing a song only the redeemed can sing. Heaven's concert is interrupted by the sounds of approaching hoof beats. The four horsemen now ride as Christ the Lamb begins to break the seals of the book. The praise and worship are now suspended for a time as the Tribulation Period begins to unfold and the wrath of the Lamb is revealed upon the earth.

I.   **The Rider On The White Horse (1-2)**
1. Many confuse the rider on the white horse as being that of Jesus Christ.
   A) This rider has a bow, Christ has a sword.
   B) This rider has a crown (stephanos), Christ has many crowns (diadema).
   C) This rider is a great imitator of Christ but he is a liar, he is the Antichrist.
2. He comes with a bow, but has no arrows.
   A) He comes on a platform of peace and unity.
   B) Daniel 9:26-27 – He makes a covenant to protect.
   C) 2 Thessalonians 2:3-12 -- Many will believe lies.
   D) The Antichrist will break his covenant in the middle of the Tribulation Period (week of years) and turn on Israel.
3. The world is set to accept and receive just such a person who claims he can bring peace.
   A) Professor A.J. Toynbee, Director of Studies in the Royal Institute of International Affairs said, "By forcing on mankind more and more lethal weapons and at the

same time making the whole world more and more interdependent economically, technology has brought mankind to such a degree of distress that we are ripe for deifying any new Caesar who might succeed in giving the world unity and peace."

B) Leaders push for a one world government.

C) The Humanist Manifesto drawn up in 1933 and updated in 1973 is being taught in many classrooms promoting humanist religion.

D) There is today much talk of peace and the way is now being paved for the so called peacemaker to come to the throne as a world dictator.

E) Matthew 24:5

II. The Rider On The Red Horse (3-4)

1. The peace promised by the false, self acclaimed peacemaker does not last.

   A) This peace was only temporary.

   B) This peace was counterfeit like its author.

2. This will be the war of all wars with untold blood-shed.

3. Matthew 24:6-7a

4. Everyone running for office promises peace.

5. The storm clouds are now on the horizon as we face what might be World War III.

6. Russia and her allies are going to invade the nation of Israel according to Ezekiel 38-39.

III. The Rider On The Black Horse (5-6)

1. "…there will be famine…" (Matthew 24:7)

2. This rider represents famine and economic disaster.

3. It has been stated by many that famine and war go together.

4. This rider has a pair of scales in his hand.

   A) "To eat bread by weight" is a Jewish phrase showing the scarcity of food.

B)   Food will most likely be rationed in this time.

5.   A man's daily wage will only buy enough of the poorest food for his own needs.

6.   Today half the children of the world that are of pre-school age are undernourished which retards their physical and mental growth.

7.   Statistics:

A)   More than half the world goes to bed hungry.

B)   Everyday in the United States we throw enough food into our garbage cans to feed a family of six in India.

C)   Fifteen percent (15%) of all edible food in the United States ends up in the garbage; this is at acost of $17.5 billion annually.

D)   While we sit down for dinner 400 people will starve to death.

E)   Each new day there are 203,000 additional mouths to feed, each year 74,000,000 more the net increase of births over deaths.

8.   "...do not damage the oil and the wine." (v.6)

A)   The rich will continue to indulge in the luxuries.

B)   The luxuries of the rich will be untouched.

IV.   The Rider On The Pale Horse (7-8)

1.   Famine, war, and the disease, pestilence ultimately lead to death.

2.   This rider is on an ashen, sickly pale horse.

A)   Authority was given to him over one fourth of the earth.

B)   He would kill with the sword, famine, pestilence and wild beasts.

a)   Twenty (20) million died in the influenza epidemics of WWI.

b)   Six (6) million died of the typhus epidemics of WWI.

c)   Aids and other STD's of today could claim millions.

      d)   There is enough bacteria stockpiled to infect untold numbers of people. There are chemical agents that can destroy an entire population. The biological weapons and nerve gases that are available can penetrate the clothing and skin.

      e)   Someone has suggested that the beasts might be the small rat who can carry 35 different diseases. The fleas of the rat were responsible for the bubonic plague and can carry typhus. It is said if you wipe out 95% of the rat population, it will replace itself in one year.

   C) One and one half to two billion people will die.

3.   Do we understand the total meaning of death?

   A) Hades -- This is the place where the souls of the lost go.

   B) Spiritual Death -- separation and rebellion against God (ex: Adam).

   C) Physical Death -- Death of the body.

   D) Eternal Death -- Eternal separation from God.

Conclusion:

The Tribulation Period is going to be a time like the world has never seen or known. God said except the days be shortened no life would be saved. But those days will be shortened for the sake of the elect.

The White Horse -- Deception
The Red Horse -- Destruction and Division
The Black Horse -- Despair and Disaster
The Pale Horse -- Death

If the Lord should return this day, would you be ready? Are you absolutely sure of your position in Christ? Where will you be when The Lamb begins to break the seals upon the scroll that is sealed?

THE DAY OF THE WORLD'S GREATEST PRAYER MEETING
<u>MEETING</u>
<u>REVELATION 6:9-17</u>

The four horsemen of the apocalypse have made their way throughout the earth and now the Lamb begins to break the fifth and sixth seals of the book. The fifth seal begins the midway point of the Tribulation Period. The full wrath of the Lamb is now going to intensify and be poured out upon the earth. Christ spoke in the Olivet Discourse of the events now taking place in Matthew 24:9 regarding this fifth seal.

He also spoke in Matthew 24:10-13 regarding the things spoken of when the sixth seal is open.

I. **The Martyred Remnant (9-11) (Fifth Seal)**
    1. The position of the tribulation martyrs (9)
        A) They are "*underneath the altar.*"
        B) They are with the Lord and are secure.
        C) The blood of the Lamb is the reason for their position of safety.
    2. The perseverance of the tribulation martyrs (9)
        A) They were faithful in their testimony unto death.
        B) They were faithful in their proclamation of the Word of God unto death.
        C) The Antichrist hates the Word of God as does Satan because it is "TRUTH!"
    3. The persecution of the tribulation martyrs (9)
        A) They were slain because of the Word of God and their testimony. They experienced great hostility.
        B) 2 Timothy 3:12 reveals to us that all who desire to live godly in Christ Jesus will be persecuted.

C) This is a time when the true redeemed will be revealed. They remain faithful.

4. The prayer of the tribulation saints (10)
   A) Psalm 64:7-9
   B) Psalm 79:10
   C) Psalm 94:1-4
   D) *"Cried out"* -- (krazo) an urgent need or strong emotion.
   E) Their prayer is not one of vengeance but one that longs to see the holiness and justice of God vindicated.

5. The possession of the tribulation martyrs (11)
   A) *"White robe"*
   B) This is a symbol of the righteousness given to them by the Lamb.

6. The patience of the tribulation martyrs (11)
   A) They are told to rest a little while longer.
   B) God has decreed that there are others who like them will be faithful unto death.

II. The Mysterious Rupture (12-17) (Sixth Seal)

1. The physical changes of creation.
   A) At this point we see all of nature is out of joint. There are drastic changes in the heavens.
   B) *"The sun became black...."* (12)
   C) *"The whole moon became like blood..."* (12)
   D) *"The stars of the sky fell to the earth..."* (13)
   E) *"The sky was split apart like a scroll..."* (14)
   F) *"Every mountain and island were moved out of their places..."* (14)
   G) This is perhaps the reason for the earthquake that is mentioned in verse 12; all things stable shaken.
      a) Revelation 6:12
      b) Revelation 11:13
      c) Revelation 16:18-19

2. The persons that are involved in this calamity (**15a**)
   A) The kings of the earth
   B) The great men
   C) The commanders
   D) The rich
   E) The strong
   F) The slave
   G) The free man
   H) There is no one that is excluded. These were not repentant as others will not be. They do not repent but they curse God.
3. The pleas of mankind (15b-16a)
   A) Mankind will hide in caves and among the rocks of the mountains trying to flee the wrath of the Lamb.
   B) There will be no place to escape and death will not come (Revelation 9:6).
   C) Vance Havner said the day will come when the most expensive piece of real estate will be a hole in the ground.
4. The presence of the Lord (16b-17)
   A) The presence of the Lamb is terrifying to the lost.
   B) To try and escape His presence and wrath will be an impossibility.

Conclusion:

Mankind should come to the Lamb while He is still dealing with man according to His mercy and grace. To wait until there is a more convenient time is a foolish and unwise decision.

THE SURVIVORS & MARTYRS

REVELATION 7:1-17

The events that are described in this chapter happen at a later time in the book of Revelation. The time will come when Satan will launch an all out war on the Saints who belong to Christ. God is giving us a snapshot preview of what He will do in caring for those who belong to Him. There will be those who are sealed and protected during the time of the Great Tribulation while others will face martyrdom because of the Word of God and their faithful testimony for Christ.

There are two distinct groups mentioned in this chapter. We find the 144,000 that are sealed and protected from the attack of the Beast and we find a multitude before the throne who have given their lives for the sake of Christ. Someone has put it this way: "There is the sealing of God's servants on earth and the singing of God's servants in heaven."

I. **The Storm That Is Imminent (1-3)**
    1. The angels of God stand in the corridors of the heavens awaiting the time in which they will carry out God's judgments.
    2. It is the calm before the storm when God will use nature to judge the people of the earth.
    3. The angels of God are given some control over the forces of nature as we see them "holding back" the four winds of the earth which represent the judgments that are to come.
        A) Holding Back (krateo)
        B) Struggling to break free
    4. These servants of God are told not to harm the earth or sea until God's bond servants are sealed.
        A) Seal (sphragis) (protection, possession)

    B)   2 Corinthians 1:22; Ephesians 1:13-14
5.   There is a stark contrast between these who receive the seal of God and those who receive the mark of the Beast.
    A)   Revelation 13:17
    B)   Revelation 14:11
    C)   Revelation 16:2
    D)   Revelation 19:20

II. The Sealed Jews of Israel (4-8)
1.   The number sealed is 144,000.
2.   Twelve tribes of Israel: 12,000 from each tribe.
3.   The question is often raised, "Why is Levi included and why is Dan and Ephraim excluded?"
4.   Many believe that Dan and Ephraim are excluded because of their idolatry and spiritual adultery. This is a hard and difficult question to answer.
5.   This is a time that describes the national salvation of Israel (Zechariah 12-13).
6.   These 144,000 are to be God's evangelists as they go forth with the Gospel. The multitude we find in the latter part of this chapter could very well be the fruit of their labors. It has also been suggested that those we find standing before the throne are the result of the two witnesses of Revelation 11.

III. The Saved Gentiles That Are Innumerable (9-17)
1.   They are no longer rejected but received. **(9)** "*Standing before the throne*"
2.   They are reaping victory. (9) "*Palm branches were in their hands*"
3.   They are counted righteous. (9) "*Clothed in white robes*"
    A)   White (leukos) shinning, dazzling
    B)   Robe (stole) a full length robe
4.   They are rejoicing. (10-12)
    A)   "*They cry out with a loud voice…*"

     B)   This praise is not temporary but eternal.
5.   They are redeemed. (13-14) *"They have washed their robes…blood"*
6.   They are rewarded. (15-17)
     A)   They have the privilege to serve. (15)
     B)   They have a protection that is secure. (15)
     C)   They have no more persecution to suffer. (16)
     D)   They have no more pain or sorrow. (17)
     E)   They have the Lamb as their Shepherd. (17)

Conclusion:

It goes without saying, God is a protector of those who belong to Him. The sealed and the saved in this chapter both are identified with the Lord. Some He sealed and others He rescued through martyrdom.

The persecution during the time of the Tribulation will be horrific. Should Christ come today for His church many would be left to face the judgments of God, those we know and love. Do you have any unfinished business regarding your witness for Christ?

This chapter is somewhat of an interlude or parenthetical statement which seems to indicate the calm before the storms begin. The seventh seal is yet to be opened. At that time things will become more intense and unprecedented Tribulation will be poured out like the world has never seen. May we find ourselves busy about the Lord's work while it is still day.

With this seal being opened the trumpet judgments will soon begin. Looking back we have seen the first six seals which were opened.

1. The False Christ (6:1-2)
2. War (6:3-4)
3. Famine (6:5-6)
4. Death (6:7-8)
5. Martyrs (6:9-11)
6. Physical Changes of Earth (6:12-17)

With the opening of the seventh seal comes unprecedented terror, horror, and judgment. Satan's rule is about to come to a close with the out pouring of God's wrath and judgment. The seventh seal contains the seven trumpets. The trumpet judgments will take place during the last half of the Tribulation Period. Some scholars tell us that the trumpet judgments will take place in the first half of the Tribulation Period. These judgments will intensify as they unfold. One can notice that the trumpet judgments are similar to the plagues God sent on Egypt.

I. The Transition Marked By Silence (1)
1. There is a heavenly hush and a pause which marks a calm before the chaos is unleashed.
2. This is a transition from grace to judgment.
3. Why the silence?
    A) The book is now completely open.
    B) All of heaven now sees the judgments that are about to be poured out.
    C) All of heaven stands in awe at what they see.

    D) There had been praise and worship to the Father and the Lamb, but with the opening of the last of the seven seals heaven now pauses in silence.

4. "The Lord is in His holy temple. Let all the earth be silent before Him" (Habakkuk 2:20).

II. The Trumpets And Their Significance (2)

1. Trumpets have always played an important role in Israel's history:
   - A) Call an assembly
   - B) Started the procession moving
   - C) Sounded for war
   - D) Feasts days
   - E) To anoint and enthrone the king
2. "I was in the Spirit on the Lord's day, and I heard behind me a loud voice like the sound of a trumpet" (Revelation 1:10).
3. Revelation 4:1 reveals how John was called up to heaven at the sound of a trumpet.
4. One day the trump of God will sound and the church will be raptured to meet the Lord in the clouds in the air (1 Thessalonians 4:16).

III. The Triumph of The Saints (3-4)

1. Another angel stands with a golden censer with much incense.
2. There is no question that this is speaking concerning prayer.
3. Twice each day the priest would take hot coals from the altar into the Holy Place and would ignite the incense.
4. Incense symbolizes the prayers of God's people.
5. Revelation 6:9-11 tells us the martyred saints are about to be vindicated as God answers their prayers as He upholds His holy Law.
6. The cries of God's children go up into His presenceand from these the trumpet judgments will go forth.

IV. The Thunder And The Sounds (5)

1. The silence in heaven of about a half hour comes to a close for judgment is about to resume.
2. The angel takes the censer filled with fire and throws it to the earth.
3. Like fire that fell on Sodom and Gomorrah God's judgment is hurled out of heaven to earth.
4. The judgment is God's answer to the prayers of the saints.
5. Thunder signifies the coming of the storm. (4:5, 8:5, 11:19, 16:18 - catastrophe)
6. Lightning follows thunder and the earthquake is a result of God's judgment on the earth during the Tribulation Period.

V. The Trumpets To Be Sounded (6)

1. The angels of God stand ready at His command to sound the trumpets that will usher in an awesome time of judgment.
2. The judgments that follow are not symbolic as some have concluded; these judgments are literal.
3. The storm is about to begin in an answer to the prayers of the saints.
4. Remember those of Revelation 6:16 who had hid themselves.
5. About the time the calm and silence end they will surface from beneath the rock and from the caves only to be met with the terrors of the trumpet judgments.

Conclusion:

The Tribulation Period will be a time of unparalleled horror and devastation such as the world has never seen. Nothing will compare to what lies ahead for those who are left to face this dreadful time. There will be a period of three and one half years of a literal hell on earth to fall on mankind. Where will our loved ones be? Where will our friends and co-workers be? WHERE WILL YOU BE?

WHEN THE TRUMPETS SOUND
REVELATION 8:7-13

As the war trumpets begin to sound the Day of the Lord is realized in its fullness. Judgment is poured out on creation and man like the world has never seen nor will ever see again. This unparalleled time of judgment will be a time of amazement, shock, terror, and awe for those who dwell upon the earth. The seven trumpets will give way to the seven bowls that will be poured out later.

I. **Destruction On The Earth (7)**
1. With the sound of the first trumpet hail and fire that are mingled with blood are thrown to the earth.
2. Plant life was first to be created, now it is the first to be destroyed.
3. The green vegetation of the earth is the target of the judgment now being issued out.
    A) Trees – refers to the fruit trees
    B) Earth – soil ruined, no crops, the oxygen supply
    C) Green Grass – pasture lands, animal life
4. This is similar to the seventh plague God brought on Egypt (Exodus 9:18-26).
5. The world's greatest ecological disaster will take place with the first trumpet.
6. The hail and fire could be the result of the earthquake spoken of in Revelation 8:5.

II. **Devastation In The Seas (8-9)**
1. This reminds us of the first plague God sent upon Egypt (Exodus 7:19-21).
2. The seas cover about three fourths of the earth's surface.
3. Imagine the devastation of this judgment.
    A) One third of the sea creatures die.

    B)   One third of the ships are destroyed.

    C)   Food supply, oxygen supply is affected.

4.   "Something like a great mountain burning with fire."

    A)   This could be a meteorite of some form.

    B)   God throws with force some great mass into the sea resulting in a catastrophic judgment.

    C)   When this great mass, whatever it might be is thrown into the sea great tidal waves will swallow up one third of the ships and their cargo.

5.   With the first trumpet God judges the land and with the second trumpet He judges the seas.

III. Death In The Rivers (10-11)

1.   With this trumpet the fresh water is polluted which results in the contamination of all drinking water.

2.   Man is dependent on water for survival.

    A)   One third of the rivers and springs are touched in this judgment.

    B)   The drinking waters will be so polluted that many will experience death.

3.   "A great star…like a torch…"

    A)   Star (*aster*) – This could be any celestial body other than the sun and moon.

    B)   Torch (*lampas*) -- fiery debris

4.   This star evidently comes apart and distinguishes as it spreads into the various waters and rivers.

5.   Wormwood (*apsinthos*)

    A)   This word is mentioned eight times in the Old Testament.

    B)   The word refers to bitterness, poison, and death.

6.   The first two trumpet judgments had a profound affect on the daily provisions of food, but how long can man live without water.

7. Death now flows in the rivers and streams.

IV. Disaster In The Skies (12-13)

1. These activities in the heavens are somewhat similar to the ninth plague that struck Egypt (Ex. 10:21-22).
2. Struck or Smitten (*plesso*)
   A) "Plague" is derived from this word.
   B) This plague of darkness will not be permanent for God will cause great and devastating heat to be given from the sun (Revelation 16:8-9).
3. With the sun and moon darkened:
   A) Temperature changes will occur.
   B) Plant life, food growth will be affected.
   C) Will there be an energy crisis at this time?
   D) All of nature will experience radical changes.
4. Jesus said there would be signs in the heavens during the Tribulation Period.
   A) Matthew 24:29
   B) Mark 13:24-25
   C) Luke 21:25
5. "It will come about in that day, declares the Lord, that I shall make the sun go down at noon and make the earth dark in broad daylight" (Amos 8:9).
6. As the lights grow dim God has a strange messenger who proclaims three future woes.
   A) The last three trumpets to sound.
   B) Revelation 9:1-21; 11:15f
   C) "Woe" speaks of judgments and destruction that is yet to come.
7. "Those who dwell on the earth."
   A) These earth dwellers are not believers.
   B) They have rejected the Gospel.

    C) Revelation 13:8 tells us that these who dwell on the earth will worship the beast.

    D) These will eventually meet death because they refuse to repent and receive Jesus Christ as Lord.

Conclusion:

God's creation in the beginning was perfect in every way. Sin came and with it followed judgment. As these trumpets sound terrifying judgments come upon the earth. Now is the time to sow the seed of God's Word into the hearts of men that they might be saved and escape the horror ahead.

<u>**THE DEMONIC DEATH SQUAD**</u>
<u>**REVELATION 9:1-12**</u>

It is now time for the fifth angel to sound the first trumpet of woe. Remember the trumpets are set in two groups. The first four deal with judgment to the earth while the last of these seven trumpets are called three woes. With this fifth trumpet comes what some commentators have called weird and wild things. How do we describe and interpret what we find in this passage of Scripture? The problem is no doubt one of interpretation. Do we look at this passage literally, symbolically, or spiritualize it in some way? It will help to view Scripture as a whole and let the rest of Scripture be the commentary for this passage.

I.   **The Opening of The Pit (1-2)**
1.   The word "*fall*" is not in the present tense but it is in the past tense "fallen" (Revelation 12:7-9).
2.   This star that has fallen to the earth must be Satan.
    A)   Ezekiel 28:12-16
    B)   Isaiah 14:12-15
    C)   Luke 10:18
    D)   Satan who is now in heaven lies accusing the brethren will lose his access to God and be cast to the earth during the Tribulation Period.
3.   The pit referred to here may be hades but not hell.
    A)   Pit – abussos
    B)   This is literally called the "pit of the abyss" or the "shaft of the abyss."
    C)   This term is found nine time in the New Testament and each time it refers to a place to hold or restrain certain beings that have come under the judgment of God.

    D) Revelation 20:1-3 tells us that Satan will be cast into the abyss and bound for a 1000 years during The Millennial Reign of Jesus Christ.

4. The sun and air will be darkened by the smoke.

II. The Overpowering Demons From The Pit (3-6)

1. There is no doubt that men's hearts would fail them fear if they could now see these horrible creatures which rise up out of the shaft of the abyss.

2. The plague of locust like creatures is reminiscent of the seventh plague that was brought upon the Egypt (Exodus 10:4-5, 12-20).

3. This demonic death squad will invade the earth once they are released from the recesses of the earth.

    A) Many believe these creatures are fallen angels.

    B) 2 Peter 2:4

    C) Luke 8:31 (The Demoniac)

4. These demonic beings receive their instructions.

    A) They cannot hurt the grass nor any green thing, nor any tree.

    B) They can only hurt (torment) those who do not have the seal of God on their foreheads for a time of five months.

    C) They are not permitted to kill anyone.

    D) Their torment was like the sting of a scorpion when it stings a man.

5. This will be an agonizing time for those who have rejected Christ and they will seek death and it will not come to them. There will be no escape.

III. The Overwhelming Appearance of The Demons From The Pit (7-10)

1. *"They were like horses prepared for battle.."*

    A) They were battle ready.

    B) This may speak of their strength and their speed.

2. *"On their heads appeared to be crowns like gold..."*
    A) Crowns may speak of their ability to conquer.
    B) The term used for crown speaks of victory.
3. *"Their faces were like the faces of men..."*
    A) This is speaking of intelligence.
4. *"They had hair like the hair of women..."*
    A) Attractiveness
    B) This implies a seductive influence.
5. *"Their teeth were like the teeth of lions..."*
    A) This speaks of their cruelty.
    B) The lion rips and tears its prey.
6. *"They had breastplates like breastplates of iron..."*
    A) They will be impossible to resist.
    B) They will be powerful and cannot be conquered.
7. *"Their wings were like the sounds of chariots, of many horses rushing to battle."*
    A) The idea is given that no one will escape the torment from this demonic hoard.
    B) Rapid movement is implied.
8. *"They have tails like scorpions, and stings...men"*
    A) Their time to torment is limited to five months.
    B) They will inflict great pain on many who have not the seal of God on their foreheads.

IV. The Overseer of The Demons From The Pit (11-12)
1. These demonic beings have a king over them. Literal locusts do not.
2. The angel of the abyss:
    A) Abaddon – Destruction
    B) Apollyon – "The Destroyer"
3. John 10:10 states, "The thief comes only to steal and kill and destroy..."

4. Some say this is not Satan for he is only associated with the pit when he is cast into it (Rev. 20:3).
5. However, it seems clear that the destroyer or the one who causes destruction is synonymous with Satan.

Conclusion:

"The first woe is past; behold two woes are still coming after these things…" It is not over. It will only intensify as more judgments follow with the next two trumpet blasts. There has been no day like this day the Scripture speaks of. This will be a dreadful time when the earth is invaded by these demons from the bottomless pit. Have you ever wanted to die? That will be man's desire during these days.

<u>"THE DEMONIC INVASION FROM THE EAST"</u>
<u>REVELATION 9:13-21</u>

As the sixth trumpet sounds John hears a voice from the four horns of the golden altar that is before God. This trumpet of course is the second woe of the three that had been proclaimed by the great eagle flying in mid-heaven (8:13). Judgment has increased to a fever pitch with great intensity. With the fifth trumpet came demonic locusts-like creatures from the abyss. Now with the sixth trumpet comes another demonic invasion. Many believe and see this event as the Battle of Armageddon because of the great loss of life.

I.   **The Sixth Trumpet (13)**
1.   John hears the sixth trumpet sound.
2.   This signals the second of the woe judgments of the last three trumpets.
3.   These trumpet judgments come because of the prayers of the martyrs.
4.   Revelation 8:3-5; Revelation 6:9-12
5.   The prayers of God's servants are being answered.

II. **The Selected Tormentors (14)**
1.   This is the first time that we meet these four angels.
2.   It is understood that these angels are bound because they are wicked and evil.
3.   "And angels who did not keep their own domain, but abandoned their proper abode, He kept in eternal bonds under darkness for the judgment of the great day" (Jude 6).
4.   2 Peter 2:4

III. **The Significant Territory (14)**
1.   This area of the Euphrates is significant because it is the cradle of civilization.

2. This river is the boundary line dividing east and west.
3. This area is very significant because:
   A) The Garden of Eden was here.
   B) The first sin was committed here.
   C) The first murder was committed here.
   D) The first martyr died here.
   E) Babylon arose in this area and Judah was in exile.
4. It is here evidently that God will bring sin to its finality.

IV. The Specific Time (15)

1. God has fixed in His own time when this judgment will fall upon man.
2. *"The hour and day and month and year..."*
   A) There is an exact moment known by God alone.
   B) "The" hour in the NAS not "a" hour in the KJV is the better translation.
   C) The Sovereign Lord causes all things to happen according to His will and in His time.
3. God has an unfulfilled purpose and plan that will be unveiled in His time.

V. The Special Task (15-19)

1. These angels are ready and waiting to unleash judgment on the earth.
2. Unnatural demon like spirits numbering 200 million will advance under the leadership of these four angels that are loosed.
3. Their task is to kill one third of mankind.
4. In Revelation 6:8 over one fourth of the population of the earth has already been slain. This now means that at least one half or more of the population has been killed.
5. John gives a description of these demonic beings.
   A) The riders have breastplates the color of fire, hyacinth, and brimstone.

      B)   The heads of the horses were like a lion and fire; smoke and brimstone came out of their mouths.

      C)   Their power is in their mouths and in their tails.

6.   It is obvious these are not humans on horseback.

7.   It is very possible that these 200 million warriors of demonic beings came from the abyss as the locusts of the fifth trumpet.

VI. The Shocking Tragedy (20-21)

1.   While God is judging the earth in severity there will be many who in their stubborn pride will refuse to repent and turn to God.

2.   It is conceivable that those killed will be those who have taken the mark of the Antichrist, having at some previous time rejected Jesus Christ.

3.   It is also possible that those who have remained loyal to themselves and undecided about Christ will also die.

4.   It is shocking that man will persist in his sin.

5.   Notice man's sins:

      A)   Demon worship and idolatry.

         a)   Satan has always desired and sought worship.

         b)   This sin is a violation of the first and second commandment.

      B)   Murders

         a)   This will be the chief crime of the Antichrist.

         b)   This sin is a violation of the sixth commandment.

      C)   Sorceries (pharmakeia)

         a)   This speaks of drug use which will be rampant.

         b)   Drug use is always prevalent in demonic or satanic activity.

      D)   Immorality (porneia)

         a)   This speaks of all illicit sexual activity.

         b)   This too goes hand in hand with satanic worship.

E) Theft (klemmaton)
   a) Cheating and stealing
   b) This sin is a violation of the eighth commandment.

Conclusion:

"The heart is deceitful above all things, and desperately wicked: who can know it?" **(Jeremiah 17:9)**

God has already done all that is possible to reveal His great love to mankind in the gift of His Son (John 3:16). God is not willing that any should perish but that all would come to repentance and be saved. Many say, "What man needs is a second chance." It seems to be evident by the Scripture that a second chance will not move the heart of some men. If the events and judgment of the Tribulation Period do not cause man to seek God, nothing will.

<u>"THE DAY CHRIST PUTS HIS FOOT DOWN"</u>
<u>REVELATION 10</u>

We may recall in Revelation 5 the book with the seven seals. The Lamb came and took the book and began to break the seals of the book. As He broke the seals of the book the judgments of God began to be poured out upon the earth in what we know as the Tribulation Period. There was an interlude between the sixth and seventh seals of the book (7:1-17). When the seventh seal is opened there are seven trumpet judgments revealed. There is now another interlude (10:1-11) between the sixth and seventh trumpets. At this point we are again confronted with another book referred to as the little book. This book is possibly the same as the one in Revelation 5. This book contains the remainder of the judgments John the apostle is to proclaim.

I. **The Appearance of The Angel (1)**
    1. The angel is clothed with a cloud.
        A) God directed the children of Israel by a cloud (Exodus 16:10).
        B) Jesus ascended to heaven on a cloud (Acts 1:9).
        C) Jesus will return on a cloud (Revelation 1:7).
    2. A rainbow was upon his head.
        A) The rainbow was a sign of God's covenant not to destroy the world again by a flood.
        B) In judgment God remembers mercy.
    3. His face was like the sun.
        A) Revelation 1:16
        B) Radiance and glory are spoken of here.
    4. His feet were like pillars of fire.
        A) Judgment is going forth consuming that which is unholy and ungodly.

B) Revelation 1:15
5. Scholars differ as to who this strong angel may be.
   A) Some see the angel as Christ.
   B) Some see the angel as one like the others of the trumpet angels.
6. The argument is based on the word "another" in the first verse (10:1).
   A) Revelation 10:1 – "another" (allos) meaning of the same kind.
   B) "Heteros" (grk) meaning another one of a different kind. Some believe this word would have been used had this angel been that of Christ.

I. The Activity of The Angel (2-7)
1. What He holds (**2**)
   A) He has a little book in his hand.
   B) The Lamb took the book from the One on the throne (Revelation 5:7).
   C) The book contains the judgments of God.
2. Where He stands (**2**)
   A) Right foot on the sea, left foot on the land.
   B) Judgment will come to the entire earth.
   C) It is God who is sovereign and the whole earth is His and the fullness thereof (1 Cor. 10:26).
   D) Satan's rule is coming to an end.
3. How He speaks (**3**)
   A) He Speaks with the voice of a lion roaring.
      a) Satan roars to frighten.
      b) This is a roar of victory.
   B) He speaks with the voice of thunder.
      a) Thunder speaks of the storms of judgment.
      b) Thunder here can speak of majesty, power, and authority.

4. What He speaks
   A) John is told to seal up what was said by the seven peals of thunder. (**4**)
      a) Daniel 8:26-27
      b) Could it be that the judgments revealed to the apostle were so terrifying that he is told not to write them down?
      c) There is no need for humanity to speculate and try to discern what was said. God said, "Do not write," so we are evidently not to know.
   B) The angel speaks an oath. (**5-6**)
      a) God is affirming His word.
      b) The Creator is the emphasis given to John at this time.
      c) God swore by Himself regarding His covenant with Abraham (Hebrews 6:13f).
      d) Time or Delay
      i   Time is no more.
      ii   God will delay no longer, judgment will no longer be held back.
   C) When the seventh trumpet sounds the mystery of God will be finished. (**7**)
      a) The truth is hidden to those who are unsaved.
      b) The truth is revealed to God's children.

II. The Action of The Apostle (8-11)

1. John is to possess or procure the book. (**8-9**)
   A) John is commanded to take the book.
   B) This command is an individual responsibility for all of God's children to take hold of the Word of God.
2. John is to partake of the book. (**10**)
   A) *"Take it and eat it."*

       a)   It will be sweet. God's promises to us are as sweet as honey as are His assurances.

       b)   It will be bitter. God's judgments are bitter.

  B)   Ezekiel 3:1-3

  C)   Make the Word a part of the inner man.

  D)   His Word is bread, milk, meat, and honey as is symbolized by the Word of God.

  E)   Job 23:12; John 8:31

3.   John is to prophesy from the book. (**11**)

  A)   No one can share what they do not take in.

  B)   John is to warn of the coming judgments.

  C)   There is a day coming when the final trumpet will sound and time will be no more.

  D)   There is hope as God now patiently waits, come.

THE TWO WITNESSES OF GOD
REVELATION 11:1-14

We are still in the interlude between the sixth and seventh trumpet. This interlude will close at Revelation 11:14. The setting for these events of Revelation 11 is the city of Jerusalem where Israel is worshipping again in the restored temple. God's Word speaks of the temple in Ezekiel 40 and the city of Jerusalem in Zechariah 2. At this point we find ourselves at the midway point of the Tribulation Period.

I. **The Measuring of The Temple (1-2)**
    1.   The history of the Jewish temple:
        A)   Solomon's Temple
        B)   The temple rebuilt after the Babylonian exile.
        C)   The temple was defiled by Antiochus Epiphanes.
        D)   Herod's Temple
        E)   Temple was destroyed in 70 A.D. by Titus.
    2.   The temple is rebuilt when we come to Revelation.
        A)   Daniel 9:24-27
        B)   Matthew 24:15
        C)   2 Thessalonians 2:1-13
        D)   Currently the Dome of the Rock occupies the sight (Mt. Moriah).
    3.   To measure something is to claim it for yourself. (Warren Wiersbe)
    4.   God is once again going to began to deal with His people, Israel.
    5.   Instructions for measuring:
        A)   The Temple
        B)   The Altar
        C)   The people who worship within.
        D)   The outer court is left out.

6. The city will be trodden under foot for a period of forty two (42) months (1260) days.
    A) Three and one half years.
    B) The divisions of the Tribulation Period.

II. The Ministry of God's Two Witnesses (3-4)

1. The length of their ministry will be 1260 days. (**3**)
    A) This ministry takes place during the first half of the Tribulation Period.
    B) The city is tread under foot 42 months, the second half of the Tribulation Period.
    C) Their message is twofold.
        a) Repent
        b) Return to God.
2. The loyalty of their ministry (**4**)
    A) Two olive trees – two lampstands
    B) The vision which Zechariah had (Zech. 4).
        a) Joshua and Zerubbabel
        b) These represent the priesthood and prophetic ministry.
        c) These two witnesses are lights in the midst of darkness, enabled by the power of the Holy Spirit to carry out their ministry assignment as they proclaim God's faithfulness.

III. The Marks of Their Ministry (5-6)

1. The devour their enemies in a supernatural way.
2. They have the authority to bring about drought during the three and one half years.
3. They have the power to turn the water into blood (Moses and the plagues on Egypt).
4. They have the power to strike the earth with plagues.
5. These two witnesses will counteract the lying signs and wonders of the Antichrist.

IV. The Martyrdom of God's Two Witnesses (7-10)
1. As their testimony is finished the beast (Antichrist) will ascend from the abyss.
   A) The Antichrist will make war against them and kill them.
   B) The Antichrist will not permit their bodies to be buried.
   C) Sodom is symbolic of pollution, immorality, and rebellion and rejection of God.
   D) Egypt is symbolic of pride, materialism, and also oppression.
   E) Jerusalem is where the Lord was crucified.
2. The earth rejoices over the death of God's two witnesses and celebrate.
   A) They send gifts to one another.
   B) This turns in to a Satanic holiday.
   C) They were tormented by the Word; because of their wicked lifestyle they could not endure the Word of God.

V. The Miraculous Resurrection of The Two Witnesses (11-14)
1. They are miraculously raised after three and one half days (Resurrection).
2. "Come up here!" – This is seen by some as a type of the Rapture (Ascension).
   A) This is a confirmation that they belong to God.
   B) This is a confirmation they are God's servants.
3. Great fear falls upon those who are watching and see this miraculous event. This is possible for the whole world to see with today's technology.
4. Earthquake
   A) A tenth of the city is destroyed.
   B) Revelation 6:12 – Earthquake
   C) Revelation 16:18-20 – Earthquake
5. Seven thousand people are killed by the earthquake.

A) One fourth of the population was slain when the fourth seal was opened.
B) One third of the population was killed when the sixth trumpet sounded.
C) Now there are 7,000 more killed.

6. "And except those days should be shortened, there should no flesh be saved..." (Matthew 24:22)
7. There is a remnant that gives glory to God. Whether it be from remorse or repentance we do not know.

<u>**THE SEVENTH TRUMPET**</u>
<u>**REVELATION 11:15-19**</u>

As we come to the seventh trumpet we come to the end of the interlude from Revelation 10:1-11:14. It is interesting to note that there has been an interlude between the sixth and seventh seal with Revelation 7 and there will be an interlude with the seventh bowl judgment at Revelation 16:15.

We may recall in Revelation 8:13 John spoke of three woes that were to take place. In Revelation 9:12 the first has past and in Revelation 11:14 the second woe has ended. John tells us when the seventh trumpet sounds the mystery of God will be finished.

The seventh trumpet sounds in Revelation 11:15 but its judgments are not seen until Revelation 15. Beginning with Revelation 12 through Revelation 14 John looks back through the Tribulation and approaches the seventh trumpet in a different direction.

I. **The Reign of Christ (15-17)**
    1. "The kingdom of the world *has become* the kingdom of our Lord…"
        A) Satan's kingdom will come to an end.
            a) Jesus in the Gospel of John spoke of Satan as the ruler of the world.
            b) John 12:31; 14:30; 16:11
        B) Satan's kingdom involves the kingdom of the Antichrist as well.
        C) "*Has become*"
            a) John speaks as describing something that has already taken place.
            b) Christ's reign will be one with no end.
            c) Luke 1:31-33

2. Those who represent the believers are giving praise and are filled with joy.
3. This praise also is given to Jesus due to His power.
4. Zechariah 14:9 "And the Lord will be King over all the earth; in that day the Lord will be the only one, and His name the only one."

II. The Rage of The Nations (18a)

1. The world system today shows an intense hatred for God and those things related to Him.
2. God has been gracious and merciful sending His Son and offering forgiveness.
3. The world has for the most part rejected God.
4. The hatred for God and His children is seen in this chapter earlier in the incident of the two witnesses as they are killed.
   A) The world will not accept God's message.
   B) The world will not accept God's messengers.
5. Man has always wanted to go his own way and live his own life.
6. There will come a day when all the nations in their rage will gather and do battle against the Lord.
7. Revelation 19:19-21

III. The Ruling of The Lord (18b)

1. "*Your wrath came*"
   A) John speaks as before as if this event has already taken place.
   B) He sees this as having been accomplished.
2. "*The time came*"
   A) Time – (kairos)
   B) Season, era, occasion, event
3. The dead to be judged
   A) Judgment Seat of Christ (1 Corinthians 3:9-15; 2 Corinthians 5:9-11; Matthew 25:21-40)

B) Great White Throne (Revelation 20:11-15)
4. *"Reward your bond servants the prophets."*
  A) Prophets may also refer to the Lord's servants.
  B) "Saints" represent the redeemed of the Old and New Testaments.
  C) He rewards those who fear His name.

IV. The Reassurance of The Lord (19)

1. The promise of God
  A) The Ark of the Covenant
  B) This is a reminder of a covenant keeping God.
  C) He is forever faithful.
  D) The ark speaks of His presence (communion) and His promises.
2. The punishment of God
  A) *"Flashings of lightning...hailstorm."*
  B) Heaven is the source of blessings and is also the source of judgment and wrath.
  C) **Revelation 4:5; 8:5; 16:17-18**
  D) Greater judgment is coming to those who dwell on the earth.

Conclusion:

With the sound of the seventh trumpet the time has come for the Antichrist to be revealed and take his place. He will come promising peace yet he will deceive and destroy many.

Let those who have ears to hear, hear what the Word of God proclaims. Receive Christ and avoid the awesome judgments that are to come.

<u>**"SIGNS IN HEAVEN"**</u>
<u>**REVELATION 12:1-17**</u>

The seventh trumpet has sounded but we do not see the results until Revelation 16. The seals have been broken and the trumpets have sounded and the bowl judgments are to come. However, in Revelation 12-13 we are introduced to some of the main characters in this apocalyptic drama. An unholy, satanic trinity is going to appear before our very eyes. Satan, the Antichrist, and the false prophet make up this unholy trinity. Satan has always desired the worship of man and in pride sought to usurp God and His throne. The Antichrist will try to typify Christ and perform great signs and wonders and will deceive many in the process. The false prophet will do what the Holy Spirit does as he promotes the worship of the beast.

Chapter 12 looks into the past and ahead into the future.

I.   The Woman (1-2)
    1.   Her clothing.
        A)   The sun and the moon (object of light: glory)
        B)   Genesis 37:9-11
        C)   The woman is the symbolic representation of Israel from which the Messiah came.
        D)   Romans 1:3 "Concerning His Son, who was born of a descendant of David according to the flesh."
    2.   Her crown.
        A)   A crown of twelve stars
        B)   Genesis 37:9; 35:22-26
        C)   Twelve stars are the symbolic representation of the twelve tribes of Israel.
    3.   Her cry.

A) The nation is many times compared to a woman in the Old Testament.

B) "As the pregnant woman approaches the time to give birth, she writhes and cries out in her labor pains, thus were we before you, O, Lord." (Isaiah 26:17)

C) Isaiah 66:6-9

D) We must remember God's promise to the patriarch, Abraham. The world would be blessed through the seed of Abraham which ultimately speaks of the Messiah, Jesus Christ.

II. The Red Dragon (3-4)

1. His description.

    A) *Great* – power
    B) *Red* – bloodshed, murder (John 8:44)
    C) *Dragon* – serpent, adversary, vicious attacks
    D) *Seven heads* – wisdom (also 7 kingdoms)
    E) *Ten horns* – power
    F) *Seven diadems* – authority

2. His demons.

    A) One third of the angels followed Satan in his rebellion.
    B) Isaiah 14:12-15

3. His destruction.

    A) Revelation 12:4; 12:13; Daniel 7:27
    B) Satan has always been ready to destroy God's promised One. From Genesis in the Garden of Eden, at His birth, and at His crucifixion Satan thought he had captured victory.

        a) Pharaoh: In Exodus 29:3 He is referred to as a dragon or monster.
        b) Nebuchadnezzar: In Jeremiah 51:34 He is referred as a dragon or monster.

4. Parallel passages to consider:

A) Daniel 7:23-27 (fourth beast with ten horns)

B) Revelation 13:1 (The beast, 7 heads, 10 horns, 10 crowns)

C) Revelation 17 – The great harlot has 7 heads and 10 horns.

III. The Child (5-6)

1. His birth comes through Israel as God had promised. (This is the Messiah, Jesus Christ)

2. He is caught up to God, referring to His ascension (now seated on the Father's right hand).

3. He will rule the nations.
   A) Revelation 11:15; 19:15
   B) Psalm 2:9

4. After the birth the woman flees into the wilderness.
   A) God will give divine protection during the Tribulation Period.
   B) Matthew 24:15-16
   C) 2 Thessalonians 2
   D) Daniel 9:27

5. In the middle of the Tribulation Period there will be a spirit of anti-Semitism such as the world has never seen.

6. Satan has great hatred for the Jewish people.(illus. – the history of the Jewish people and their persecution)

IV. The Archangel (Michael) (7-12)

1. The conflict. (**7**)
   A) Michael and his angels wage war against Satan and his forces.
      a) The church has been raptured at this point.
      b) There is war in the heavenlies.
      c) There will be war on earth.
   B) Michael is also identified in Daniel 10:10-21 and Daniel 12:1.

C) Deuteronomy 34:5-6; Jude 9: Satan disputed with Michael about the body of Moses.
D) The name Michael means, "Who is like God?"

2. The conquest. (**8-9**)
A) Satan and his angels were not strong enough to overcome Michael and his army of angels.
B) This event marks the end of Satan's rule in the air as no place is found for them in heaven.
C) Satan's access to God's throne as the accuser of the brethren will end and he will be cast down to the earth.

3. The celebration. (**10-12**)
A) Satan will no longer be the principality and power of the air.
B) He will now be limited to earth and all of heaven will rejoice.
C) This will be the beginning stage of Christ's reign and kingdom as Satan is cast out of the heavens to the earth.
   a) They overcame by the blood of the Lamb.
   b) They overcame by the word of their testimony concerning Jesus Christ.
   c) They overcame because they were more concerned for the glory of Christ rather than for their own life (Matthew 16:25).
D) While heaven rejoices earth will experience the fury and wrath of the dragon as he realizes that his time is short.
E) Remember the woes of Revelation 8:13.

V. The Remnant And Israel (13-17)

1. Satan when cast down will begin a terrible persecution of the woman who gave birth to the child. (**13**)
2. As God's chosen people Satan has forever hated the Jewish race.

3. Exodus 19:4 tells us that God delivered Israel from the bondage of Egypt "on eagle's wings."
   A) Supernatural protection, refuge, and security will be provided.
   B) Time, times, and a half time refer to 3 ½ years.
4. *"Water like a river...flood."* (**15**)
   A) This may refer to false teaching that comes from Satan and his cohorts for his is nothing but a liar.
   B) This flood may also symbolize great armies that come against Israel when the Antichrist breaks his covenant with Israel in the middle of the week.
5. *"The earth helped the woman...mouth.'* (**16**)
   A) The rebellion of Korah (Numbers 16).
   B) This is a possible earthquake God sends to destroy the enemies who rise up against Israel.
6. Those who were not carried away will experience the wrath of Satan. They are identified as:
   A) The rest of her children.
   B) They keep the commandments of God.
   C) They hold to the testimony of Jesus.

Conclusion:

Satan's consistent wrath and diabolical hatred seems to know no end when it comes to those who profess Christ as Lord and Savior. The past history of the Jewish people and the nation of Israel regarding persecution pales in comparison to what is to come. Knowing his time is short, Satan will be more devastating and destructive than anyone can begin to imagine. War, bloodshed, and murder will be his agenda and no one who names the name of Christ will be excluded during this terrible time we know as the time of Jacob's trouble. Where will you be? Will you be among those who are raptured when the church is taken? Will you be left behind seeking a place to escape the wrath of the blood thirsty red dragon?

There is hope is Jesus Christ today. God tells us that today is the day of salvation. Why would you wait until it is too late? Come today!

<u>"THE DEVIL'S CHILD"</u>
<u>REVELATION 13:1-10</u>

Revelation 13 introduces us to an individual that is well known to the student of God's Word. This person is called the Antichrist. This name which many know to refer to a specific person is not found within the pages of Scripture. However, it is used to speak of those who deny God, His Son, and the coming of Christ in the flesh. The Antichrist will be an individual who is opposed to everything represented by God and His Son Jesus Christ. There are many other names given in Scripture to speak of the Antichrist:

Daniel 7:8; 8:9   The Little Horn
Daniel 9:26   The Prince that shall come
Daniel 8:23   A king of fierce countenance
2 Thessalonians 2 The man of sin, son of perdition, the wicked one

Within Scripture it is not difficult to see the contrast between the Antichrist and the Lord Jesus Christ. Dr. Charles Larkin, in his book *Dispensational Truth* states some of the contrast found in Scripture:

1. Christ came from above – John 6:38. Antichrist will ascend from the pit – Rev. 11:7.
2. Christ came in His Father's name – John 5:43 Antichrist will come in his own name – John 5:43
3. Christ humbled Himself – Philippians 2:8. Antichrist will exalt himself – 2 Thess. 2:4
4. Christ was despised – Isaiah 53:3; Luke 23:18. Antichrist will be admired – Rev. 13:3-4.

5. Christ will be exalted – Philippians 2:9. Antichrist will be cast down to hell – Isaiah 14 Revelation 19:20.
6. Christ came to do His Father's will – John 6:38. Antichrist will come to do his own will – Dan. 11:36.
7. Christ came to save – Luke 19:10. Antichrist will come to destroy – Daniel 8:24.

This of course is not an exhaustive list but it is clear to see that the Antichrist is everything Christ is not. However, the world is ready to receive a powerful and influential leader who promises to bring peace.

I. The Advent of The Antichrist (1)

1. *"I saw the beast coming up out of the sea..."*
    A) Sea
        a) Some interpreters see this as the Gentile nations (Revelation 17:15).
        b) Others see this as the abyss, a place of satanic activity.
        c) Others see this as a sea of people which is similar to the nations of people.
    B) This could help in identifying his nationality.
        a) Daniel 9:26 refers to, "the people of the prince." (Royal lineage – Roman)
        b) Daniel 11:36-37 states he, "Regarded not the God of his fathers..." (Jewish)
        c) Daniel 8:8-9 refers to the "Little horn" which came from four Grecian horns.
        d) Roman Grecian Jew
2. The beast is summoned by the dragon who stands on the sand of the seashore.
3. 1 John 2:8
4. Daniel 7:23

5. The Antichrist will come as a man indwelt by and with demonic power.

II. The Attributes of The Antichrist (1b-2)
1. *Ten horns*
    A) Horns speak of power.
    B) Represents rulers who rule at the same time.
2. *Seven heads*
    A) These are successive world empires.
    B) Egypt, Assyria, Babylon, Medo-Persia, Greece, Rome.
    C) Some see this as the five kings to John's time and Domitian the current ruler, then the kingdom of the Antichrist.
3. *Ten diadems*
    A) Royal crowns, legal authority
    B) Victorious power
    C) Also speaks of the world's military power and political strength.
    D) Daniel 7:7, 24
4. Body like a leopard
    A) Greek Empire (Daniel 7)
    B) Swift to conquer
5. Feet like a bear
    A) Medo-Persia Empire (Daniel 7)
    B) Strength
6. Mouth like a lion
    A) Babylonian Empire (Daniel 7)
    B) Ferocious
7. Power of the dragon
    A) Antichrist's kingdom will be an embodiment of all the previous kingdoms.
    B) Antichrist will share Satan's throne.
8. The Antichrist will be energized by hell itself.

III. The Amazement Caused By The Antichrist (3)
1. *"...his fatal wound was healed..."*
   A) The beast in some way will be slain during the Tribulation Period.
   B) The beast will gain great popularity when he is resurrected.
   C) After this unique counterfeit act of Satan many will be deceived and follow after the beast.
2. This is the greatest counterfeit ever staged by Satan.
3. This is going to be one of the dragon's greatest lying wonders.

IV. The Admiration For The Antichrist (3b-4)
1. *"They worshiped the dragon...they worshiped the beast..."*
2. Satan will achieve what he has always wanted at this point, that is worship.
   A) Matthew 4:9
   B) Luke 4:7
3. The deceived worshipers will see the Antichrist as a deity.
4. Satan's ultimate goal to receive worship has now become a reality.

V. The Attitude of The Antichrist (5-6)
1. The Antichrist will speak blasphemous insults with all arrogance.
2. Keep in mind God is in complete control as we can read, "There <u>was given</u> to him..."
3. In Daniel 7:8 we are told that the Antichrist will have a mouth uttering great boasts; he will also speak against the Most High (Daniel 7:25).
4. He will blaspheme God's name.
   A) God's person
   B) All that God is relating to His attributes.
5. He will blaspheme God's tabernacle.

A) Heaven
B) This is the place from which Satan has been removed.
6. He will blaspheme God's saints in heaven.
   A) Believers who are secure in heaven.
   B) Satan nor the Antichrist can harm them.
7. The Antichrist will have authority to act for forty two months.

VI. The Attack of The Antichrist (7)

1. The Antichrist will make war with the saints as persecution will increase severely.
2. Revelation 12 – He will also persecute Israel during this time as the world experiences an anti-Semitic crusade by the Antichrist on the Jewish people.
3. We have seen Satan's attack throughout history.
   A) Satan – Job
   B) Herod – John the Baptist
   C) Herod – Killing the babies to get to Christ.
   D) Pilate – Christ
4. Satan's thirst for the blood of God's people will be unquenchable.
5. The Antichrist will experience victory and overcome them.
   A) He will overcome them physically.
   B) He will not overcome them spiritually.

VII. The Acceptance/Adoration of The Antichrist (8)

1. Those who have not placed their faith in Christ will be deluded by the masses.
2. Unbelievers whose names are not written in the Lamb's book of life will bow their knee to a false Christ (2 Thessalonians 2:4).
3. "I have come in My Father's name, and you did not receive Me, If another comes in his own name, you will receive him." (John 5:43)

4. Don't be deceived, Satan is not opposed to religion. He is the author of every false cult that exists today.
5. His goal is to lead as many as possible away from the True Christ.

VIII. The Admonition To The Believers (9-10)

1. We are given a call to spiritual discernment, "If anyone has an ear, let him hear."
2. During the Tribulation Period there will be believers who are destined for captivity/prison.
3. Retaliation from believers is not to take place. This is true for today as well.
4. The saints then and now are to be examples of Jesus Christ as He endured persecution, yet He did not open His mouth.
5. Persecution and captivity will be the believer's lot during the days of the Tribulation Period.
6. "Therefore, those who also suffer according to the will of God shall entrust their souls to a faithful Creator in doing what is right." (1 Peter 4:19)

Conclusion:

Satan will have his time and his day. However, God is faithful to His word. Revelation 11:15 states, "The kingdom of the world has become the kingdom of our Lord and of His Christ; and He will reign forever and ever."

Satan desires to be God. It was for this reason that he was cast out of heaven. The beast from the sea is identified as the Antichrist. Now the beast from the earth comes on the scene who is a counterfeit of the Holy Spirit. We now have before us an unholy trinity, Satan, Antichrist, and the False Prophet.

I. **The Advent of The False Prophet (11)**
    1.   "Beast coming up out of the earth."
        A)   An apostate Jew
        B)   Counterfeit of the Holy Spirit
        C)   Some kind of religious leader
    2.   "And he makes those who dwell on earth to worship the first beast, the Antichrist." (13:12)

II. **The Attributes of The False Prophet (11b)**
    1.   The two horns speak of power.
    2.   He appears like a lamb gentle and harmless.
    3.   He speaks like a dragon (12:9).
    4.   He is a wolf in sheep's clothing.

III. **The Authority of The False Prophet (12)**
    1.   He derives his power from the first beast, the Anti-Christ.
    2.   He causes those who dwell on the earth to worship the first beast.
    3.   Not only is the Antichrist driven by the forces of hell but the false prophets is as well.
    4.   Horns speak of power. (13:11)

IV. **The Actions of The False Prophet (13-17)**
    1.   He is cunning (v. 13). He performs great signs.
    2.   He is charming (14a). He is deceptive.

---

3. He is creative (14b-15). He gives life to the image.
4. He is cruel (15b). He kills those who refuse to worship the image of the beast.
5. He is controlling and commanding (16-17).
    A) He compels worship. (12, 15) – Daniel 3:1-7
    B) He controls commerce. (16-17)
        a) No seal no sale.
        b) Those who take the mark of the beast are forever doomed.

V.   Acknowledgement of The Beast (18)
1. This is a call for spiritual understanding.
2. Six (6) is the number of man, who is imperfect.
3. (666) we now have perfect imperfection.

Conclusion:

The unholy trinity is now seen in its entirety. Satan's desire has always been to be worshiped. He has now achieved his purpose and in so doing has deceived mankind. His goal is also to kill, steal, and destroy.

The Tribulation Period will be a time marked by deception and murder.

<u>VISIONS OF THE LAMB WITH THE 144,000</u>
<u>REVELATION 14:1-5</u>
<u>*(SINGING WITH THE SAINTS)*</u>

The scene now shifts from that of the unholy trinity with Satan and his cohorts to the Lamb and the 144,000. The 144,000 spoken of here are those previously seen in the seventh chapter of the Revelation. These are now presented in heaven with the twenty four elders and the cherubim. They are described as the first fruits unto God and the Lamb.

I. **Saints That Are Sealed (1)**
1. Revelation 3:12 (Church of Philadelphia)
   A) The name of My God.
   B) The name of the city of My God.
   C) My new name.
2. Ephesians 1:13 (The seal of the Holy Spirit)
3. Revelation 7:4
   A) The seal is a symbol of ownership.
   B) Those who worship the beast also have a seal, but they also have no hope.

II. **Saints That Are Singing (2-3)**
1. Psalm 100
2. Revelation 5:9
   A) This is a song of redemption.
   B) We have been purchased.
   C) The purchase price was extremely costly, for it was the blood of the Lamb, Jesus Christ.
   D) People who are sealed have something to sing about.
   E) It is only the redeemed who can sing this song.

III. **Saints That Are Saved/Secure (3b)**

1. The Christian is saved, sealed, and secure.
2. John 10:28-29
3. Jude 24
4. 1 Peter 1:3-5
5. 2 Timothy 1:12
6. Philippians 1:6
7. These Scriptures show that this is not a perseverance of the saints but a preservation of the Savior.

IV. Saints That Are Separated (4)

1. *"These are the ones who have not been defiled with women…"*
2. *"For they have kept themselves chaste…"*
3. *"They follow the Lamb wherever He goes…"*
4. 2 Corinthians 6:17
5. 2 Corinthians 11:2
6. John 14:15-21 – keep His commandments

V. Saints That Are Sincere (5a)

1. The system of the beast is based on nothing but a lie.
    A) 2 Thessalonians 2:11
    B) John 8:44
    C) In Genesis 3 in the beginning Satan is seen deceiving and lying. That is his nature.
2. The saint of God has the nature of the Savior.
    A) There are no lies.
    B) There is no deception.
    C) Truthful, faithfulness, dependability.

VI. Saints That Are Spotless (5b)

1. *"They are blameless."*
2. Luke 16:10
3. 1 Peter 1:18-19
4. Ephesians 5:27

5. We can be spotless and blameless because our Lord is spotless and blameless as the Word reveals.

Conclusion:

The saints of God are a people who not only have something wonderful to sing about but something wonderful to share. His name is Jesus!

GOD'S LAST CALL: "IS THAT YOUR FINAL ANSWER?"
REVELATION 14:6-13

In chapters 12-13 a view of the Tribulation Period is given to us from Satan's perspective with the Antichrist and the False Prophet. Chapter 14 brings into view the final judgments of the Tribulation Period and the return of Christ.

Today we live in an age when we hear the Gospel of grace preached. Mankind today has a blessed privilege afforded him in hearing the good news. However, a greater privilege is one of responding positively to the Gospel message by saying "yes" to Jesus. There is coming a time in the very near future when God will make His final call which will come during the time of the Tribulation Period. It is best for man to hear and respond today to the message of the Gospel of grace. This is true, for in the days of the Tribulation Period God will send upon them a deluding influence so that they will believe that which is false (2 Thess. 2:8-12).

In Revelation 14:6-13 we see three angelic messengers of God as they deliver various messages from God to those living in the final hours of the age.

I. **The Preaching Angel (6-7)**
    1. The message delivered by this angel is one of deliverance.
    2. The angel is flying in midheaven.
        A) Midheaven – (*mesouranema*)
        B) Apex, high point at noon
        C) At this point the angel would be most visible to all people.
        D) Satan, the Antichrist, and his demonic army have been grounded at this point and confined to earth. For that reason they are not able to stop the message as the angel preaches the eternal Gospel.

3. Eternal Gospel
    A) Gospel – Good News brings eternal life.
    B) This Gospel is all inclusive; every nation, tribe, tongue and people.
    C) The message comes in a loud voice.
    D) God not only wants all to see (midheaven) but He wants all to hear (loud voice).
4. The Message
    A) Fear God – reverence (beginning of wisdom)
    B) Glorify God – honor, thanks, praise
    C) Worship God – (Psalm 19:1-4; Roman 1:18-20; Colossians 1:13) Worship Him as Creator.
5. Jesus said the Gospel would be preached to the whole world and then the end would come.
6. The seal and the trumpet judgments which have brought devastation to the earth have been experienced.
7. Now the message is that the "Hour of judgment has come."
    A) Judgment (*krisis*) refers to wrath.
    B) The bowl judgments are about to be poured out.
8. So, this preaching angel brings God's call of grace and mercy to an unregenerate world, calling them to repentance.

II. The Pronouncing Angel (8)
1. The message delivered by this angel is one of disaster.
2. Although many will hear the proclamation of the Gospel and be saved the message will for the most part will be rejected.
3. Notice another followed in sequence with the mess-age of judgment concerning Babylon.
4. This is the first mention of Babylon in Revelation.
5. Babylon
    A) The economic, political, and religious system of the Antichrist.

B) Babylon throughout Scripture has always shown herself as an enemy of God.
C) Babylon is a symbol of evil, idolatry, and rebellion (Genesis 11 – The tower of Babel).

6. In the end times Babylon will hold a great influence.
   A) Nations will drink of the wine of the passion of her immorality.
   B) Passion (*thumos*) consuming lusts and desires
   C) Immorality is spoken of here in reference to the spiritual idolatry of the people.

III. The Predicting Angel (9-13)

1. The message this angel delivers is one of doom and damnation.
2. A holy, righteous, and just God is going to deal with sin.
3. God has graciously given this final call to sinners to repent during this final hour.
4. Now the angel announces the doom and damnation for those who persist in their worship of the beast and his image.
5. Those who worship the beast, his image, and receive his mark will drink of the wine of the wrath of God.
   A) Full strength means an undiluted judgment.
   B) This judgment is not tempered with grace.
   C) There will be no element of grace, mercy, or compassion.
6. These deceived followers of the Antichrist:
   A) Are tormented with fire and brimstone.
   B) Find no rest day or night.
   C) Find that hell is eternal without end.
   D) Suffer before the holy angels and the Lamb. There is no place that the Lord is not; He is omnipresent.

7. Those who on the other-hand reject the Antichrist will be martyred but the beasts' efforts are all for naught. God will translate the faithful martyrs to glory (14:12-13).

Conclusion:

Three angelic messengers sound God's last call. God in His great love continues to pursue man until the last hour. Man is stubborn in his rebellion against God. However, God is just as stubborn in His love for man and in His grace gives man one final opportunity to repent before final judgment falls.

The Gospel message goes forth from a loving God. Will you receive His Son and be born again? _____________

Is that your final answer?

The harvest of the end times is a time of separation. Several Old Testament prophets spoke of this time and the Lord coming in judgment. In fact some of the same analogies are used by the Old Testament prophets as those found in this passage of Revelation. For instance, Joel 3:12-13 states, "Let the nations be aroused and come up to the valley of Jehoshaphat, for there I will sit to judge all the surrounding nations. Put in the sickle, for the harvest is ripe. Come, tread, for the winepress is full; the vats overflow, for the wickedness is great." The prophet Isaiah also uses the same picture of judgment as he describes the Lord carrying out His judgment as He trods the winepress alone (Isaiah 63). Christ spoke of the harvest that would take place in the parable of the "Wheat and Tares" (Matthew 13:36-42).

In this passage of Revelation we find what appears to be two harvests. In Revelation 14:15 it is stated that the harvest of the earth is ripe which refers to the grain harvest. In Revelation 14:18 it is stated that the grapes from the vine of the earth are ripe. It would appear that the Apostle John is giving the reader a glimpse of judgment in two different areas. First of all, he refers to the grain harvest. John is perhaps referring to the seven vials or bowl judgments that are yet to be poured out which are found in Revelation 16. In reference to the grape harvest, Revelation 14:20 helps us to identify this harvest as the coming battle of Armageddon which is found in Revelation 19. Therefore, it seems that John is letting us see the finality of God's judgment in the seven bowls and also the battle of Armageddon.

I.   **The Harvest of Grain (14:16)**

1. The Christ and The Cloud (**14**)
    A) The occupying the cloud is the Lord Jesus.
        a) Matthew 24:30
        b) Daniel 7:13-14
    B) The cloud speaks of His majesty and glory.
    C) In this passage we see Him as the One reaping; He has the sharp sickle.
        a) Matthew 13 -- Jesus is the Sower.
        b) Matthew 13 -- "The Wheat and Tares"
    D) "Son of Man"
        a) This is Jesus' favorite title for Himself.
        b) Matthew 8:20 is the first time we see it used.
    E) He has a golden crown upon His head.
        a) Crown -- (stephanos)
        b) This is the victor's crown in war.
        c) Christ has come to destroy His enemies and reign forever.
2. The Angel and The Announcement (**15**)
    A) This angel comes out of the temple. This is the fourth angel in Revelation 14.
    B) This lets us know that the announcement or the message comes from God.
    C) The angel speaks with God's authority, crying in a loud voice which speaks of urgency.
3. The Hour and The Harvest (**15**)
    A) The hour of God's judgment has come.
    B) The harvest of the earth is ripe.
        a) It is overripe, rotten, dried up, withered.
        b) It is no longer useful.
    C) Grace and mercy have come to an end and God will delay no longer.
    D) As it was in the days of Noah, God's Spirit will not always strive with man.

4. The Savior and The Sickle (**16**)
    A) The Sovereign Lord now executes judgment.
    B) In quick fashion He swings the sickle of judgment and the earth is reaped.
    C) In Revelation 16 John gives the details of this judgment regarding the harvest of grain.

II. **The Harvest of Grapes (17-20)**
    1. The Angel and The Assignment (**17**)
        A) He has a sharp sickle.
        B) He comes out of the temple as the angel before.
        C) This fifth angel will assist in the judgment of the unbelievers who survive the bowl judgments.
        D) Angels as seen previously in Revelation assist greatly in God's work and judgment.
        E) This angel operates under God's authority.
    2. The Angel and The Altar (**18**)
        A) This sixth angel has power over fire.
        B) This sixth angel has come from the altar.
            a) The priest would take hot coals morning and evening from the altar.
            b) The coals were used to burn incense in the Holy Place.
        C) Revelation 6:9-11; Revelation 8:3-5
        D) The prayers of the saints are ready to be answered.
        E) This angel gives the order for judgment to be executed.
            a) *"...her grapes are ripe..."*
            b) The term used here means fully ripe, at their prime, wickedness is full, the ultimate rejection of God has taken place.
    3. The Angel and The Accumulation (**19**)
        A) The angel swings the sickle and the clusters (the unredeemed) are gathered and thrown into the

winepress.
B) The winepress is the place of God's wrath.
C) This will be a time of separation.
D) As the golden grain is separated from the black darnel so the wicked and vile are separated from those who belong to God.

4. The Winepress and The Wrath of God (**20**)
   A) The winepress is trodden outside the city.
      a) The city spoken of is of course Jerusalem.
      b) Revelation 16:16
      c) Revelation 19:11-21
   B) Christ will defeat all of His foes in the final battle.
      a) The Antichrist
      b) The False Prophet
      c) All of Satan's demonic army will perish.
   C) Blood will flow to the horses' bridle.
      a) This will be a blood bath.
      b) This will be a slaughter far beyond anything the world has ever seen.
      c) The destruction of human life will be massive.

Conclusion:

The harvest of grain and the harvest of grapes, are both ripe and ready for the reapers to come. Christ and His angels will be the reapers as those who do not know Christ are gathered together for the final time of judgment. Those who are unredeemed face a terrifying and horrible future with no hope. Will anyone be spared? Will anyone be saved? Is there someone you need to reach by standing in the gap?

THE JUDGMENT THAT LOOMS JUST OVER THE HORIZON
REVELATION 15:1-8

The shortest chapter in the Book of Revelation is Chapter 15. This Chapter serves as an introduction to Chapter 16 and the bowl judgments that lie ahead. This Chapter not only serves as an introduction to the days of the Great Tribulation but it also brings to a close the events concerning the visions in heaven in Chapters 10 through 15. John begins by stating that he saw another sign in heaven. John describes this sign in verse 1 as "great and marvelous" which signifies its importance since it is revealing God's final act of judgment upon the earth during the Tribulation Period. This is the third sign that John has seen. He had already seen the woman clothed in the sun and the great red dragon in Chapter 12. This sign John now sees consists of seven angels with seven plagues.

I.   **The Completed Wrath of God (1-2a)**
 1. John sees seven angels who had seven plagues.
     - A) Plague – a blow or a wound
     - B) These seven plagues will be the last and worst because "in them the wrath of God is finished."
     - C) Wrath (thumos) speaks of rage, passionate outburst of anger.
     - D) In Zephaniah 3:8 the prophet tells of God's wrath being poured out in the last days.
 2. John also saw a sea of glass.
     - A) In Revelation 4:6 John mentions a sea of glass before the throne.
     - B) This shining sea of glass like crystal may be similar to what the prophet Ezekiel saw in his call vision as he

speaks about an awesome crystal gleam and an expanse.

C) The sea of glass was mixed with fire.

    a) Many see the fire as the trials endured by the tribulation saints.

    b) Others see the fire as God's judgment to come.

II. The Committed Worshipers of God (2b-4)

1. Upon the sea of glass stand the victorious saints of God.

    A) These are tribulation saints not the raptured church.

    B) They have been true to the Word of God and have maintained their testimony.

2. These have been victorious over:

    A) The beast – Political system

    B) His image – Religious system

    C) His number and name (mark) – Economic System

3. They are holding harps of God.

    A) They are rejoicing.

    B) They are praising God and singing.

4. These saints sang the song of Moses and the song of the Lamb.

    A) The Song of Moses – Physical deliverance (Exodus 15:1-18)

    B) Song of the Lamb – Spiritual deliverance (Revelation 5:8-14)

5. John Phillips in <u>Exploring Revelation</u> states that, "The song of Moses was sung at the Red Sea, the song of the Lamb is sung at the crystal sea; the song of Moses was a song of triumph over Egypt, the song of the Lamb is a song of triumph over Babylon; the song of Moses told how God brought His people out, the song of the Lamb tells who God brings His people in; the song of Moses was the first song in Scripture, the song of the Lamb is the last. The song of

Moses commemorated the execution of the foe, the expectation of the saints, and the exaltation of the Lord; the song of the Lamb deals with the same three themes." (*Exploring Revelation*, rev. ed. [Chicago: Moody, 1987; reprint, Neptune, N.J. : Loizeaux, 1991] 187)

6. The contents of the song speak of the attributes of God which Christ possesses (**vs. 3-4**).
   A) Creator – "Great and marvelous are Your works, Lord God Almighty."
   B) Righteous – "Righteous and true are Your ways"
   C) Worthy of worship –"King of the nations…glorify Your name."
   D) Holy – "for You alone are holy."
   E) Eternal – "All nations will come…revealed.'

III. The Commanding Will of God (5-8)
1. *"After these things."* (**v. 5**)
   A) John appears to have another vision (Rev. 11:19).
   B) His vision involves the seven plagues or bowl judgments described in Revelation 16.
2. The tabernacle of testimony of heaven is opened and the judgment that awaits the unredeemed masses of humanity is now revealed .
   A) Temple: here refers to the Holy of Holies.
   B) Temple is mentioned 15 times in Revelation.
3. Seven Angels (**vs. 6-8**)
   A) Seven plagues – Revelation 16, bowl judgments
   B) Clothed in linen, clean and bright – purity and holiness.
   C) Golden sashes – beauty and majestic dress, the idea is that of being dressed for judgment.
   D) Seven golden bowls – (phialas) shallow saucer
   E) The bowls are filled with God's wrath.
4. The temple is filled with the smoke.

    A)   God's glory (dedication of Solomon's Temple) is made manifest.

    B)   God's power is revealed.

5.   *"No one was able to enter..."* (**v. 8**)

    A)   Access to God is cut off.

    B)   No angel, human being will enter God's presence until judgment upon the earth is complete.

    C)   When man refuses mercy then judgment follows.

    D)   God's glory stands guard barring the way into the Holy of Holies.

Conclusion:

Scholar, John Phillips once stated, "Since Calvary the way into the holiest of heaven has been opened to all, because the blood of Christ has blazed a highway to the heart of God. But now for a brief spell, that royal road is barred."

Imagine; no access to heaven. Can you fathom a time when it will do no good to pray?

Why not seek God now while He may be found.

<u>GOD'S FINAL ACT OF JUDGMENT</u>
<u>REVELATION 16</u>

Revelation 15 served as an introduction to Revelation 16 and the pouring out of the seven bowls. The last days of the Tribulation Period are now taking place. The first three and one half years have come to a close and God is brining to a close the time of Jacob's trouble as He rescues the world and rids it of evil. The wrath of God against sin is displayed in these final acts of judgment on an unbelieving world. When these bowl judgments are completed we will see the return of the Lord Jesus Christ as John describes the event in Revelation 19.

I. **The First Bowl (2)**
    1. The first bowl poured out on the earth brings loathsome and malignant sores on mankind.
        A) Sore (helkos): This is the Greek equivalent of the Latin word from which the English word ulcer comes.
        B) Loathsome – (kakos): This is the Greek word for evil, depraved, and injurious.
        C) Malignant – (Poneros): This is the Greek word for evil, diseased, malicious and grievous.
    2. This resembles the sixth plague experienced by the Egyptians (Exodus 9:8-12).
    3. "There is no relief for your breakdown, your wound is incurable. All who hear about you will clap their hands over you, for on whom has not your evil passed continually." (Nahum 3:19)
    4. Those who suffer from this judgment are those:
        A) Who have received the mark of the beast.
        B) Who worshiped his image.
    5. Revelation 14:9-11

6.   God will protect believers during this time.

II.   The Second Bowl (3)

1.   The second angel poured out his bowl into the sea.
2.   The sea became blood like that of a dead man.
3.   The first plague Egypt experienced was similar as the Nile River was turned to blood (Exodus 7:20-24).
4.   Revelation 8:8 tells us when the second trumpet sounded something like a great mountain burning with fire was thrown into the sea and a third of the sea became blood.
5.   The sea becomes corrupt and everything dies.
   A)   There is a great stench from the dead bodies of everything living in the sea.
   B)   Commercial shipping may come to a halt.
   C)   The water supply will be affected.

III.   The Third Bowl (4-7)

1.   The third angel pours his bowl out upon the springs of water and the rivers.
2.   The fresh water like that of the seas became blood.
3.   A third of the world's fresh water is affected with the sound of the third trumpet judgment. (Revelation 8:10-11)
4.   Now the entire water supply, sea water and fresh water is contaminated.
5.   God's judgment is seen as being justified.
   A)   The Antichrist will have shed much blood during the Tribulation Period.
   B)   Those who have spilled much blood will be given blood to drink.
   C)   They receive their just desserts for their wickedness. This is what we might call poetic justice.
6.   The saints who had been praying for God's justice to be done affirm His righteous acts of judgment on those who

spilled the blood of the saints and the prophets (Revelation 6:9-11).

IV. The Fourth Bowl (8-9)
1. The fourth angel poured his bowl out on the sun.
2. The first three angels pour their bowls out on the earth, the fourth angel on the sun.
3. Men are scorched with a fierce heat from the sun.
4. Remember there is no water available to quench the thirst of man.
5. Revelation 8:12 tells us that with the sound of the fourth trumpet a third of the sun was struck, yet it still produces an intense heat.
6. "There will be signs in sun and moon and stars, and on the earth dismay among nations, in perplexity at the roaring of the sea and waves" (Luke 21:25).
7. "The light of the moon will be as the light of the sun, and the light of the sun will be seven times brighter, like the light of seven days, on the day the Lord binds up the fracture of His people and heals the bruise He has inflicted" (Isaiah 30:26).
8. Revelation 13:13 reveals the false prophets made fire come down out of heaven to earth in the presence of men.
9. Even in such devastating circumstances man will blaspheme the name of God and refuse to repent and give glory to God.

V. The Fifth Bowl (10-11)
1. The fifth angel poured his bowl out upon the throne of the beast.
2. Darkness comes upon his kingdom.
3. Revelation 9:2 states when the fifth trumpet sounded the earth was darkened by the smoke that came out of the bottomless pit.
4. Many scholars have suggested different geographical locations.

A) The temple is located in Jerusalem.

B) Rome is the location of the apostate church.

C) Babylon speaks of his political system which will most likely be rebuilt during the Tribulation.

5. "But in those days, after the tribulation, the sun will be darkened and the moon will not give its light" (Mark 13:24).

6. "Alas, you are longing for the day of the Lord, for what purpose will the day of the Lord be to you? It will be darkness and not light." (Amos 5:18).

7. The ninth plague on Egypt was one of darkness (Exodus 10:21-23).

8. Joel 2:1-2 refers to this as a day of darkness and gloom.

9. Man blasphemes God and does not repent of his deeds.

A) Their pains and sores are still evident. The sores and the scorching heat are excruciating. These sores are incurable and the pain causes them to gnaw their tongues (keep on chewing).

10. Total darkness also will have a mental effect on mankind.

VI. The Sixth Bowl (12-16)

1. The sixth angel poured his bowl on the Euphrates and it waters dried up.

2. This judgment actually comes in two parts.

A) The Euphrates River dries up.

B) Demonic spirits bring armies to the valley of Megiddo.

3. The Euphrates has long been a natural barrier between the east and the west.

A) Genesis 15:8 reveals the Euphrates was the eastern border of land that God gave to Abraham.

B) The Euphrates River

a) 1800 miles long

b) 3600 feet wide in some places

c) 30 feet deep in some places

C) The Euphrates River served as the eastern border for the Roman Empire

4. *"The kings of the east"*
   A) It literally says, "of the sun rising"
   B) Oriental nations such as China, Japan, India…

5. Revelation 16:13-16: The Battle of Armageddon
   A) The unholy trinity is on the scene.
      a) The dragon
      b) The beast
      c) The false prophet
   B) These three send out demonic spirits which deceive through performing signs and lying wonders.
   C) Somehow through this deception the kings of the world are gathered together for the war of the great day of the Lord.
   D) Zechariah 12 and 14 gives us a picture of this battle from Israel's point of view.

6. Armageddon (Revelation 19:11-16)
   A) Plain of Esdraelon
   B) Valley of Jezreel
   C) Meggido – place of troops or place of slaughter.
   D) This valley is 14 miles wide and 20 miles long.

7. This valley has been a chosen place of encampment for many warriors of every nation in history. (Saul, Josiah, Gideon, Barak)

8. Napoleon Bonaparte referred to this as the ideal battleground for all the armies of the world.

9. 9. In Revelation 16:15 The Lord gives a faithful challenge. "Remain faithful the end is near."

VII. The Seventh Bowl (17-21)

1. The seventh angel pours his bowl upon the air.

A) "in which you formerly walked according to the course of this world, according to the prince of the power of the air, of the spirit that is now working in the sons of disobedience" (Ephesians 2:2).

B) Satan is referred to as the prince of the power of the air.

2. A loud voice says, "It is done."

A) *It is done* (gegonen): This stresses a completed action with ongoing results. Judgment has come to unrepentant sinners.

B) *It is finished*: Jesus at Calvary took man's judgment of sin and provided salvation for all who repent and receive Him as Lord and Savior.

3. The seventh bowl is like the seventh seal (8:5) and the seventh trumpet (11:19) as we see peals of thunder begin to sound.

4. At this time there will be an earthquake unlike anything the world has ever seen.

A) "For thus says the Lord of hosts, 'Once more in a little while, I am going to shake the heavens and the earth, the sea also and the dry land'." (Haggai 2:6)

B) Hebrews 12:26-27

5. The Great City

A) Revelation 11:8 identifies the great city as Jerusalem.

B) The city will be split into three parts.

C) Zechariah 14:4-10

6. Cities of the nations will fall, at the same time the kingdom of Antichrist, Babylon, will drink the cup of the wrath of God.

7. The islands and the mountains will disappear and be made flat.

8. Hailstones about 125 pounds will come crashing down upon the earth and humanity.

A) The seventh plague of Egypt was similar but not as intense (Exodus 9:23-24).

    B) In Revelation 8:7 the first trumpet brought hail and fire mixed with blood.
9. Imagine huge chunks of ice crashing to the earth where because of the great earthquake people are found without shelter.
10. The survivors of this plague blaspheme God.
11. Revelation 16:17 "IT IS DONE!"

Conclusion:

The Lord's admonition in Revelation 16:15 applies to all.

- Be ready.
- Be watching.
- Be clean.

In Revelation 17:1 we see one of the seven angels who had one of the seven bowls announcing the judgment of the great harlot, Babylon. This is the fall of religious Babylon. It has already been stated in Revelation 14:8 that Babylon the great is fallen. This chapter speaks of the false and corrupt religious system of the Antichrist. Chapters 17 and 18 of the Revelation show the relationship of Babylon to the beast and the world rulers and the judgment that comes upon her.

God's Word informs us that in the last days there will be a great falling away. Paul gives us the details regarding this falling away in 1 Timothy 4:1-3; 2 Timothy 3:1-3; and also 2 Timothy 4:1-4. We are living in these days at the present time when churches have compromised the message of the Gospel for fear of offending someone. We are told to find a person's needs and meet that need even if you must compromise the message of repentance and the cross. The concern for numbers and being viewed as successful has taken precedence over what thus saith the Lord. We are living in the seeker sensitive, user friendly church age. The end result is we have feel good preachers helping people go to hell with a positive attitude and a smile on their face.

So, who is this woman in Revelation 17 who rides the back of the scarlet beast? She is the mother of harlots, of idolatry and pagan worship and devotion. Remember that Satan the Dragon has a cheap counterfeit for everything God has. In Revelation we find two women. One of these women is found in Revelation 12 and now the other in Revelation 17. Notice their differences.

Revelation 12
Mother of righteousness

Revelation 17
Mother of unrighteousness

Brought forth a Son	Mother of harlots
Clothed with heavenly garments, clothed in the sun.	Clothed in purple, scarlet, gold, precious stones, pearls. Earthly garments
Moon under her feet	Rules over the kings of the earth.
Produces masculine nobility	Produces feminine impurity
Helped by celestial wings	Carried by the power of the dragon
Crown of twelve stars	Blasphemous names
Takes abode in heavenly city	Goes down to eternal ruin
Woman- Israel bringing forth the Son of God	Woman- turning hearts away from Christ to idolatry and false religion

The mother of harlots had her beginning as we read from Genesis 10 and Genesis 11. It all began with Nimrod who was the grandson of Ham. Nimrod's names means "rebellious planter." Some have referred to him as a forerunner of the Antichrist. The people followed Nimrod and desired to make a name for themselves and be independent of God. This was corporate pride. So, Nimrod in essence was the founder of a new religion which denied and blasphemed God. Does this not sound like much of today's so called religion which has totally turned away from Christ to every "ism" of the world? This spirit of Babel lives on. However, God stopped it then and Christ will stop it and abolish it when He comes in power and great glory.

I.   The Decree Concerning The Harlot (1)
1.   Judgment will come to the Babylonian mother.
2.   Revelation 17 and 18 give us details of what is being judged regarding Antichrist and his kingdom.
3.   John shows us that the judgment upon the harlot is tied to the seven bowls poured out in the previous chapter.
4.   Revelation 14:8

II.   The Description of The Harlot (1)
1.   *"the great harlot who sits on many waters…"*
2.   We find the harlot in a position of power and one of authority.
3.   Revelation 17:15 gives us the meaning of the many waters where the harlot sits.
     A)   Peoples
     B)   Multitudes
     C)   Nations
     D)   Tongues
4.   The harlot's authority and power will be worldwide.
5.   False worship will be practiced by the masses.

III.   The Domination of The Harlot (2-3)
1.   She commits acts of immorality with the kings of the earth.
     A)   Spiritual adultery
     B)   Idolatry
     C)   The world rulers will be enamored with the false religion.
     D)   Revelation 13:8
2.   *"Those who dwell on the earth"*
     A)   Unbelievers, unredeemed
     B)   They too give their hearts to the harlot thereby committing acts of spiritual adultery.
3.   *"Made drunk with the wine of her immorality"*

A) This is not literal wine but figurative language is describing how those on the earth are so deceived and taken in.

B) Jeremiah 51:7 gives similar descriptive words.

4. John's vision changes and he is carried away in the Spirit into a <u>wilderness</u>.

A) This describes a deserted, desolate place.

B) Here John sees a woman; the harlot which John heard the angel describe.

5. *"Sitting on a scarlet beast"*

A) The Antichrist is supporting the harlot.

B) False religion is riding the back of the political system.

C) Religion will unite the kingdom of the Antichrist.

D) Revelation 17:16 reveals the beast will turn on the harlot and the false prophet will promote the worship of the beast.

6. The beast: *"Full of blasphemous names."*

A) Claims to be God

B) 2 Thessalonians 2

C) Daniel 7:25

7. Scarlet is a color identified with royalty and luxury.

8. *"Seven heads"*

A) Revelation 17:9-10

B) Seven mountains, seven kings

C) This represent past, present, and future rulers.

9. *"Tens horns"*

A) Revelation 17:12

B) Ten kings, these will rule under the Antichrist.

IV. The Dress of The Harlot (4a)

1. She is clothed in purple and scarlet, and adorned in gold and precious stones and pearls.

2. It is evident that the harlot is wealthy and worldly.

3. Her colors are like that of the beast.
4. Like a worldly harlot she appears attractive and seductive.

V. The Designation of The Harlot (4b-5)
1. *"A golden cup"*
   A) The unredeemed and unbelievers will be enamored with the false religion.
   B) The idolatry is an abomination to God.
2. Babylon is symbolic of everything that is in defiance of God and His kingdom.
3. This godless system will be great in its influence throughout the world.
4. *"Mother of harlots"* speaks of idolatry and her corruption.
5. Babylon was the fountain head of the corrupt system which opposes God and all that is holy and righteous.

VI. The Deeds of The Harlot A(6)
1. The woman was drunk with the blood of the saints and witnesses of Jesus.
2. Those who refuse the mark of the beast and stand for Christ, refusing to worship the image will be persecuted and are put to death.
3. To be drunk with the blood of the saints is to say that the kingdom of the Antichrist will shed much blood in the days of the Tribulation Period.
4. Today if you desire to live godly in Christ Jesus will be persecuted (2 Timothy 3:12).
5. In the twentieth century more Christians experienced martyrdom than any other time in history.
6. There is an antichristian bias in our country today.

In Revelation 17:1-6 John sees a vision regarding Babylon, the religious harlot. In Revelation 17:7-18 we are given the interpretation of what John saw in his vision. One could say that the mystery is revealed.

Babylon is mentioned in the Scripture over one hundred times. It is mentioned thirty times in the New Testament. The term "Babylon" means confusion and stands for that which is corrupt. In this chapter we see Babylon as the false religious system of the beast. Some have even referred to it as the false church or the false bride. Without a doubt the whole system is evil and empowered by Satan as he works through the beast who is the Antichrist. So, we see Babylon as Satan's counterfeit of God's truth.

I. The Motive of The Beast (7)
1. *"...and of the beast that carries her..."*
2. Satan and the Antichrist will use the apostate religious system to gain world power.
3. Revelation 6:1-2 informs us that the Antichrist will come with a platform of peace which the world will at that time be seeking.
4. The harlot, false religion, is carried along by the beast in order that he might fulfill his own selfish and evil desires.
5. It is during this time that Antichrist will organize the European confederation of ten kings or kingdoms.

II. The Mockery of The Beast (8)
1. *"The beast that you saw was, and is not, and is about to come..."*
2. Revelation 13:3; 13:12

3. We know that the greatest miracle that has ever taken place is the resurrection of Jesus Christ our Lord on the third day following His crucifixion.
4. The greatest deception of all will be when the Antichrist somehow deludes the masses into believing that he has been resurrected from the dead.
5. 2 Thessalonians 2:9-12
6. The entire ministry of the Antichrist will be nothing but a mockery of the ministry of Jesus Christ.

III. The Mystery of The Beast (9-13)
1. *"Seven heads are seven mountains…and they are seven kings…"* (**vs. 9-10**)
    A) Mountains are used sometimes in Scripture to speak of rule or of power.
    B) These seven mountains spoken of represents seven world empires or kingdoms.
    C) John is speaking here of past, present, and future kingdoms. (John is speaking of Rome.)
2. *"…five have fallen, one is, the other has not yet come…"* (Five emperors had ruled prior to John's writing; Domitian was reigning as John wrote.)
    A) Five have fallen;
        a) Egypt
        b) Assyria
        c) Babylon
        d) Medo-Persia
        e) Greece
    B) One is: -- Rome
    C) The other has not yet come: This is the future kingdom of the Antichrist.
    D) Antichrist is the eighth and one of the seven.
3. "The ten horns…not yet received a kingdom." (**v. 12**)

    A) These are ten kings.
    B) Ten kings will rule under the Antichrist and give him the allegiance and power.
    C) Daniel 2:40-43 (ten toes); Daniel 7:24 (ten horns)
4. These receive power with the beast for "one" hour.
    A) Antichrist's kingdom will not last.
    B) "One hour" speaks of the brevity of his rule.

IV. The Mastery of The Lamb (14-18)

1. "These will wage war….faithful." (**v. 14**)
    A) The Lamb will overcome (Revelation 19).
    B) The Battle of Armageddon (Revelation 16:13-14, 16).
    C) He will have with Him:
        a) The chosen.
        b) The called.
        c) The faithful.
2. This universal influence of apostasy will be destroyed by the Sovereign and Supreme Lord.
3. God will put into the hearts of the beast and the ten kings to rise up and destroy the harlot. (**vs. 16-17**)
    A) They hate the harlot.
    B) They make her desolate.
    C) They make her naked: she is stripped of her wealth and luxury. The Antichrist is only using the religious system for his own purposes.
    D) They eat her flesh: devour her wealth.
    E) They burn her up with fire: total ruin.
4. *"Their hearts….His purpose."* (**vs. 17**)
    A) God is sovereign.
    B) God has a divine plan.
5. Babylon in her pride and wealth will no longer flourish.

Conclusion:

This corrupt religious system, the great harlot is guilty of deceit, corruption, violence, pride, and evil. Every religious system that does not bow to the blood of Jesus Christ is of the system of Babylon. These God will judge and will bring to a quick destruction.

<u>THE GREAT FALL OF BABYLON</u>
<u>REVELATION 18:1-8</u>

Revelation 17 showed us the religious aspects of the kingdom of the Antichrist. The religious kingdom of the Antichrist will come to an end as he will turn in hatred toward the religious prostitute, Babylon (Revelation 17:16). It would seem that the Antichrist will only use religion as a platform to bring himself to power until he takes his seat in the temple proclaiming himself to be God. As we see the collapse of worldwide religion in Revelation 17 we now see the collapse of economic and commercial Babylon. As religious Babylon is stripped of her possessions, wealth, and treasures so will the degradation of the economic and political Babylon be. Revelation 18 gives us the world's conditions at the time of final judgment when Christ returns to set up His kingdom. Business and government are seen as being intertwined. Therefore what affects one will affect the other.

I.   **The Proclamation of Babylon's Destruction (1-2)**
    1.   Babylon is a Satanic kingdom and will be judged. (14:8)
        A)   A dwelling place of demons (demonic activity)
        B)   Unclean spirits (corruption and abominations)
        C)   Prison of unclean and hateful birds
            a)   agents of Satan
            b)   Matthew 13:31-32
    2.   This proclamation comes from an angel coming down from heaven.
        A)   The angel has great power.
        B)   The angel has a radiant glory.
        C)   The angel is announcing God's message to Babylon.
    3.   Isaiah the prophet uses similar language and it may be that John has this on his mind as he is writing. (Isaiah 13:19-22)
    4.   Babylon's place of supremacy is lost.

5. The language suggests that Babylon has already fallen.
6. Parallel passage (Zechariah 5:5-11).

II. The Punishment of Babylon's Deeds (3-8)
1. The reasons are given for the judgment Babylon will receive.
    A) "The nations have drunk the wine of the passion of her immorality." (18:3) (Nations have been seduced to turn away form the true Christ.)
    B) "The kings of the earth have committed acts of immorality with her." (18:3; 18:9)
        a) The kings of the earth and the apostate church loves the world of wealth.
        b) 1 John 2:15-17
    C) "The merchants of the earth have become rich by the wealth of her sensuality. (18:3) (Many are looking for gain through the religious system.)
    D) Babylon's sins have piled up as high as heaven. (18:5)
        a) Genesis 11:4
        b) Babylon – system always opposed to God.
    E) "Pay her back even as she has paid...." (18:6)
        a) Revelation 17:6
        b) Persecution and martyrdom of the saints
        c) Exodus 22:4, 7, 9
    F) False confidence and pride (18:7)
        a) She glorified herself.
        b) She lived sensuously or deliciously.
        c) She saw herself as a queen who would never be dethroned.

III. The Participation With Babylon Denounced (4)
1. God calls for His people to separate themselves from the vile unclean things and practices of the world.
2. Perhaps some of God's people appeared to be close to Babylon in order that they might escape persecution and

possibly death.

3. God gave specific reasons for His people to separate themselves.
   A) The pollution caused by Babylon. (18:3)
   B) The plagues Babylon would experience. (18:4)
4. 2 Corinthians 6:14-17

IV. The Promise of Babylon's Destruction (8)

1. God has promised judgment upon Babylon and His Word will not return void.
2. Characteristics of judgment:
   A) Plagues
   B) Pestilence
   C) Poverty (famine)
   D) Purging (fire)
   E) Powerful (God is strong.)
3. Babylon's destruction will be:
   A) Sudden (18:8)
   B) Swift (18:17)
   C) Severe (18:21)

God has spoken concerning the judgment that is coming to Babylon. The Word speaks as if this judgment has already taken place. All that is opposed to God is symbolized by the political and economic Babylon.

The question often asked by many is, "Will Babylon be rebuilt?" There are many scholars who do believe that the old ancient Babylon will be rebuilt due some prophecies concerning Babylon that are unfulfilled. Tim Lahaye, in his book, <u>Revelation</u>, states," Isaiah 13 and 14 and Jeremiah 50 and 51 describe the destruction of Babylon as being at the time of the 'Day of the Lord.' A careful reading of these four chapters reveal that the prophecies concerning the destruction of Babylon in the Old Testament use the law of double reference; that is, they refer to the overthrow of Babylon the enemy of Israel in the seventieth year of their captivity. But since Babylon is the headwaters of the world's governmental, commercial, and religious systems in opposition to the will of God, the second reference in these prophecies has to do with the day of Jehovah, or the Tribulation Period." Lahaye further states, "The prophecies of Jeremiah and Isaiah indicate that 'Babylon is suddenly fallen and destroyed' (Jeremiah 51:8). Isaiah 13:19 states, 'And Babylon, the glory of kingdoms, the beauty of the Chaldeans' excellency, shall be as when God overthrew Sodom and Gomorrah.' When taken together, these two prophecies indicate that Babylon will be destroyed by a sudden cataclysm, much the same way as Sodom and Gomorrah. History reveals that ancient Babylon was never destroyed like that."

The world system today is much like the religious harlot and commercial Babylon. There is rebellion and defiance of everything that is holy and God is rejected by the world. Like Babylon this entire system will come crashing down and those who have placed their trust and security in the worldly Babylon will find themselves without hope and forever lost.

John shows us in Revelation 18 the reactions of earth and heaven regarding the fall of Babylon.

I. **The Reaction of The Earth (9-19)**
    1. The lamentation of the monarchs (**9-10**).
        A) The kings of the earth speaks of the political system.
        B) In Ezekiel 27 the prophet spoke of the fall of Tyre using similar language as John uses here.
        C) The kings of the earth had committed acts of immorality and lived sensuously with her.
        D) They stand at a distance weeping and mourning overwhelmed by her judgment and destruction that comes so quickly (one hour).
    2. The lamentations of the merchants is seen. (**11-16**)
        A) The merchants mourn because no one is left to buy their cargoes anymore. (11)
        B) There are some 28 items of trade mentioned.
        C) The luxury which for many had become a necessity are removed.
        D) Everything seems to be affected at this point.
            a) Sales are gone.
            b) Stocks are gone.
            c) Furniture industry is affected.
            d) Farming and agriculture is affected.
        E) There seems to be nothing in the economic system left untouched by God's judgment on Babylon.
    3. The lamentation of the mariners is seen. (17-19)
        A) The entire shipping industry is halted.
        B) All who make their living by the sea stand at a distance not believing that such a great city could be made so

desolate in such a short time.
C)   They like other merchants had become rich. (19)

II.   The Reaction of Heaven (20-24)
1.   There is great rejoicing in heaven because of the judgment that Babylon has suffered.
   A)   This is not a rejoicing because of their suffering.
   B)   There is rejoicing because of God's judgment is righteous.
      a)   His judgment is violent. (21)
      b)   His judgment is complete. (21)
2.   Entertainment is gone. (22)
   A)   Harpists, musicians, flute players and trumpeters are not heard any longer.
   B)   Amusement and social life are gone.
3.   Business and commercialism has ended. (22)
   A)   No craftsman of any craft is found.
   B)   Industry ceases to be, there is no business life.
4.   Family life also seems to vanish. (23)
   A)   The light or lamp does not shine any longer.
   B)   The voice of the bridegroom and the bride are not heard.
5.   There appears to be no habitation whatsoever in the city.
6.   One scholar summarized verses 21-23 by saying there is:
   A)   No city (21)
   B)   No craft (22)
   C)   No candlelight (23)
   D)   No celebration (23)
7.   Heaven can rejoice because the deception and the immorality are now judged and removed.
8.   Heaven can rejoice because the blood of the saints has been vindicated.
9.   All that man had placed his trust in is no more.

Conclusion: (Mark 8:34-38)

Of what profit will it be to you if you gain the whole world, and lose your soul?

A HEAVENLY CELEBRATION
REVELATION 19:1-10

The Book of Revelation is for many a book of mystery and misunderstanding. Many questions are asked as to what is the meaning of the seals, the trumpets, and the bowl judgments. Other questions are asked regarding the Antichrist and his identity, his mark, and when he will appear. The events of the Tribulation Period also raise many questions. Man wants to know if the church will go through the horror and devastation of the Tribulation Period. Others look for wisdom and understanding regarding the Rapture of the church. It is evident that the questions and the quest for understanding the Book of Revelation will never cease while man inhabits this earth. However, there is one event in the Revelation that we can be sure of. It is the coming again of Jesus Christ to reign and to rule over all the earth. Jesus Christ, King of kings, and Lord of lords will reign supreme and of His kingdom there shall be no end! Warren Wiersbe tells us that Revelation 19 and 20 records five key events that will take place before God wraps up human history and ushers in His new heaven and earth.

- Heaven will rejoice (19:1-10).
- Christ will return (19:11-20:3).
- Saints will reign (20:4-6).
- Satan will revolt (20:7-10).
- Sinners are recompensed (20:11-15).

Now, in Revelation 19:1-10 we have four hallelujahs and a wedding taking place. Alleluia is the Greek equivalent to the Hebrew word hallelujah. This word means, "Praise the Lord." It is a good thing to know that praising the Lord has not and will not go out of style for all eternity.

I. A Multitude That Is Rejoicing (1-6)

1. The First Hallelujah (**1**)

    A) This hallelujah comes because of salvation which belongs to God.

    B) "Behold, God is my salvation. I will trust and not be afraid; For the Lord God is my strength and song, and He has become my salvation." (Isaiah 12:2)

    C) All of heaven rejoices because salvation history is completed and the saints are now glorified in the kingdom.

    D) What God began in Christ at the foundation of the world is now being completed.

    E) Heaven can praise Him for salvation as they are free from the penalty of sin, the power of sin, and the presence of sin.

2. The Second Hallelujah (**2-3**)

    A) This hallelujah speaks of judgment.

    B) God's judgments are true and righteous.

    C) The great harlot and her corrupting influence and rebellion are brought to an end.

    D) The persecuted saints have waited and longed for the justice of God to spring forth.

    E) Isaiah 9:6-7

    F) "'Behold the days are coming, declares the Lord,'When I shall raise up for David a righteous Branch; and He will reign as king and act wisely and do justice and righteousness in the land." (Jeremiah 23:5)

3. The Third Hallelujah (**4-5**)

    A) This hallelujah speaks of worship.

    B) Throughout the Book of Revelation the twenty-four elders and four living creatures have worshipped God (**4**:10; 5:8; 5:14; 7:11; 11:16; 19:4).

    C) Amen ("So let it be" or "So be it.")

D) All of heaven seems to be in agreement realizing that God is worthy of all worship.

4. The Fourth Hallelujah (**6**)
   A) This hallelujah speaks of God's sovereign rule and fellowship with the redeemed.
   B) Revelation 11:17
   C) "The Lord reigneth; let the earth rejoice." (Psalm 97:1)
   D) Philippians 2:9-11 reveals the exaltation of Christ is coming.

II. **A Marriage Supper That Is Ready (7-10) (Oriental Wedding Characteristics: Betrothal, Presentation, Celebration)**
   1. The celebration is ready to commence. (**7a**)
      A) The marriage of the bride and the Lamb is ready to take place.
      B) The bride of Christ is the church for which He gave His life. (2 Corinthians 11:2)
      C) Jesus Christ, the Lamb, is the Groom.
      D) The church today is betrothed or engaged to Christ.
         a) Christ will return in the air to take His bride to heaven.
         b) John 14:1-3
         c) 1 Thessalonians 4:13-18
   2. The preparation of the bride is completed. (**7b-8**)
      A) 1 Corinthians 3:12-15 (The Judgment Seat)
      B) 2 Corinthians 5:10
      C) The bride is dressed "in the righteous acts of the saints."
      D) At the judgment seat of Christ all the imperfections will be removed. (1 John 3:2)
   3. The invitations to the supper are confirmed. (**9**)
      A) The invitations go out to those who are guests.
         a) This includes Old Testament saints who were saved before Pentecost.

        b)   Tribulation saints who were saved after the Rapture of the church are also included.

    B)   Believers are gathered at the banquet table at the Marriage Supper of the Lamb.

    C)   The fourth beatitude in the Book of Revelation is given to those who are invited to the supper.

4.   The glorification of the Lamb has come. (**10**)

    A)   Jesus Christ the Lamb is God.

    B)   He alone is worthy to be worshipped and praised.

    C)   He alone is the key to all prophecy.

    D)   He is the central theme to Old Testament prophecy and New Testament preaching.

    E)   All who proclaim the Gospel must be faithful to His testimony which is His message.

Conclusion:

After the Marriage Supper Jesus will present His bride with a celebration that will last 1,000 years. This is known to us as the Millennium (Revelation 20:4). There is going to be a wedding, a royal wedding with a great and glorious celebration. Are you going? Are you ready? The time to pre-pare is today. The place to prepare is here. The person to prepare is yourself.

<u>**"JESUS CHRIST RETURNS TO EARTH"**</u>
<u>**REVELATION 19:11-21**</u>

Without a doubt one of the greatest events and promises in all of the Word of God is the fact that Jesus Christ will one day return to the earth to set up His Millennial kingdom. The King of kings and the Lord of lords is coming again! He is coming to establish righteousness and rule and reign with a rod of iron.

When we pray, "Thy kingdom come, Thy will be done," we may rest assured that the answer is soon to come.

I. **Jesus Is Coming Physically (11a)**
   1. The return of Jesus will be a bodily return.
   2. The emphasis here is on what John saw.
   3. "Every eye shall see Him..." (Revelation 1:7)
   4. Until this point He has been interceding but now returns to judge.
   5. Acts 1:11
   6. Matthew 24:27-31
   7. There are many views regarding the Second Coming of Christ.
      A) Some view His Second Coming as happening on the day of Pentecost (Acts 2).
      B) There have been others who believe the Second Coming of Christ occurs when a person is born again. (Salvation)
      C) When a person experiences death and enters into the presence of the Lord is viewed as the Second Coming by some individuals.
   8. Scripture is clear on this matter that the return of Christ will be a physical bodily return.

II. **Jesus Is Coming In Power (11b-16)**

1. White horse: This speaks of one who comes in victory.
2. He will come as the One who conquers.
3. At His first coming He came to redeem but now He comes to reign.
4. At His first coming He came as Savior now He comes as Sovereign.
5. At His Second Coming He will not come do die on a tree but will take His throne.
6. He is Faithful and True. The beast (Antichrist) was a liar and deceived many.
7. He is not only the conqueror who comes as a consuming Christ.
   A) He has penetrating eyes. Nothing will escape His vision. (**v.12**)
   B) On His head is a crown (diadema). This speaks of rule and authority. (**v. 12**)
   C) His name is secret. (**vs. 12, 16**) (**Philippians 2:9f**)
   D) His robe is dipped in blood. This is the blood of His enemies. All rebellion, rejection, and immorality have come to an end. He defeats all that is ungodly and evil. (**v. 13**)
   E) Isaiah 63:3
   F) The criteria for His judgment will be righteousness, His righteousness.
   G) Christ comes and the armies of heaven who have washed their robes and made them white in the blood of the Lamb will come with Him.
   H) Jude 14-15
8. He will rule and smite the nations and take His place as Sovereign Lord to reign and rule (Psalm 2:9).
9. He is King of kings and Lord of lords.
   A) 1 Timothy 6:15
   B) Revelation 17:14

III. Jesus Is Coming To Punish (17-21)

1. Jesus is coming to do battle with His enemies.
2. The call is given and the summons to the final battle of human history.
   A) Joel 3:9-16
   B) Zechariah 14:1-13
   C) Zephaniah 1:14-18
3. The summons is also given to the birds to come and eat the flesh of kings, commanders, the slave, and the small and great. There is no escape for the ungodly and those who have practiced evil and made themselves an enemy of Christ.
4. The beast and the false prophet who had deceived many into taking the mark of the beast and worshipping him are thrown alive into the lake of fire that burns with brimstone.
   A) Matthew 13:41-42
   B) Revelation 21:8
5. The weapon of Christ will be His mighty Word.
   A) The Battle of Armageddon will not be a lengthy battle. As Christ speaks His enemies will be destroyed. His powerful word will consume them.
   B) This is a battle that will be won by a word, the powerful word of Christ.
   C) "...and with the breath of his lips shall He slay them." (Isaiah 11:4)

Conclusion:

In Revelation 19:1-10 we read of the Marriage Supper of the Lamb. This will be a supper of great joy. In Revelation 19:11-21 we see Christ coming in great power and judgment. This will be a great supper of judgment as we can see.

It is a great comfort and joy to know that Christ is your Savior and to also know which supper you will attend. The events of Revelation

19 should inspire the Christian to live godly each day. For the sinner it should lead him or her to repentance before it is too late.

THE MILLENNIAL REIGN OF JESUS CHRIST
REVELATION 20:1-10

As we have seen in Revelation 19 Jesus Christ is coming again to this earth. After the defeat of His enemies He will then establish His kingdom, the Millennial kingdom here on the earth. There is much debate and speculation when it comes to the Millennial kingdom and its interpretation. We get the term millennium from two Latin words:

- mille (thousand)
- annum (year)

It may help to define three views regarding the Millennium and Christ's kingdom.

1. Postmillennialism – This view takes the position that man and the world will continue to get better and better thereby the kingdom of God will be established and then Jesus Christ will return.
2. Amillennialism – This view sees the 1,000 years and spiritualizes it and sees Christ's victory over His enemies and the blessings for the church now that Satan has been defeated and bound. This view means there is no literal kingdom (no millennium).
3. Premillennialism – This view tells us that man will continue in his course of sin and depravity. Things will not get better and better but actually worse. Christ will return to the earth to establish His kingdom. This view treats the Scriptures literally.

The duration of 1,000 years is referenced six times in this passage:

1. Satan is bound 1,000 years. (v. 2)

2. Satan will deceive the nation no more until the 1,000 years are completed. (v.3)
3. The saints will reign with Christ for 1,000 years. (v. 4)
4. The rest of the dead lived not again until the 1,000 years were completed. (v. 5)
5. The resurrected will be priests of God for 1,000 years. (v. 6)
6. Satan will be loosed when the 1,000 years have been completed. (v. 7)

I. Satan Will Be Restrained. (1-3)

1. The angel has the key to the abyss and the power to restrain Satan and cast him into the abyss.
    A) Some view this angel as being the Lord Jesus.
    B) Revelation 1:18 tells us that He has the keys to death and hades.
    C) However, we must keep in mind that hades and the abyss are not the same.
    D) The abyss is the bottomless pit and the abode of demonic beings and spirits.
2. John again gives us the names which characterize Satan.
    A) Dragon: He causes people to behave like beasts and stirs up within man brutal passions and desires.
    B) Serpent: He seduces, deceives, beguiles, and leads people to reject and disobey God.
    C) Devil: He is a slanderer, a liar, and a murderer.
    D) Satan: He has spiritual power that opposes and accuses man. He stands as an enemy to all who choose to follow God. He also opposes God.

II. Saints Will Be Reigning. (4-6)

1. The dedicated are rewarded as they have been faithful.
2. The tribulation martyrs will be raised from the dead.
3. These have paid the ultimate price and have been totally committed (no worship, image or mark).

4. The church will also reign and rule with Christ in the Millennial kingdom. This is the believer's inheritance in Christ.
5. John saw people sitting upon thrones with the authority to rule and judge. (1 Corinthians 6:2)
6. There is a resurrection of believers only as stated in verse 5.
    A) John 5:28-29
    B) 1 Corinthians 15:23
    C) 1 Thessalonians 4:16
    D) There will be a resurrection at the introduction to the millennium.
7. They saints of God are extremely blessed and are rewarded.
    A) They are perfected into the holiness of Christ.
    B) They will not be touched by the second death.
    C) It is granted to them to reign with Christ for 1,000 years.
8. The Scriptures inform us that many nations will be in existence during the millennium.
    A) Psalm 2:6-9
    B) Micah 4:3
    C) Zechariah 14:16-19

III. Satan Will Be Released. (7-10)

1. Satan will be released at the end of the millennium and he will immediately begin to deceive the nations as he had done previously.
    A) Some who have lived in the millennium and have been a part of the perfect government of Christ will rebel against Christ.
    B) This proves that a perfect environment cannot and will not produce a perfect heart.
    C) Satan always has his loyal followers and they will be drawn back to him.
    D) Gog and Magog: the enemies of God and Christ.

2. Satan will make one last assault against Christ and His followers.
3. God is going to release Satan thereby vindicating the justice of God.
   A) Mankind will see the corruption of the human heart.
   B) There will be no one who could speak against the righteous judgment of a holy God.

IV. Satan Will Be Ruined. (10)

1. The enemy of God and His followers will meet with a sudden and swift defeat.
2. The deceiver of the ages will see his so called kingdom and domain come to an abrupt end.
3. Satan will be thrown into hell where he once again will be reunited with his cohorts, the beast and the false prophet. These two have been tormented in hell already for 1,000 years.
4. Satan and his army will once and for all find defeat.

Conclusion:

The characteristics of Christ Millennial kingdom:

- Isaiah 11
The lion will eat straw like the ox.
The wolf and lamb will feed together.
The child will lead the wild animal.
Knowledge complete
Justice for all
- Hebrews 8: 10-11 - Perfect worship of God.
- Isaiah 2:4 – Peace
- Isaiah 35 - Change in aging, no sickness, disease.
- Zephaniah 3 – No evil action between nations.
- Zechariah 14:20 – Holiness unto the Lord
- Revelation 11 – The government will change.

Once Satan is brought to an end and cast into the lake of fire the final judgment of the wicked will come.

Will you find yourself experiencing the joys of the reign of Christ in the millennium or awaiting the Great White Throne judgment to come? Are you prepared to stand before the Lamb as the books are opened? Receive Him today and confess Him publicly as Savior and Lord.

THE SINNER'S SUNSET
(GOD'S JUDGMENT DAY)
REVELATION 20:11-15

This passage speaks of the great and final judgment. Those who have rejected the Lord Jesus Christ have a "date with Deity." This is to be the end of all things. The setting is one of a courtroom; however, this will be the final court for all of eternity. There will be no appeals made or delays in the judgment that is given. Everyone will meet and face the King of kings and the Lord of lords, Jesus Christ. You will either face Him at the Judgment Seat of Christ or the Great White Throne judgment. That is a choice that you make based on what you do with Jesus Christ.

I. **The Place of Judgment (11)**
    1. "*Great*" speaks of power. This throne is far greater than any judicial bench or any supreme court.
    2. "White" speaks of purity. Jesus is perfect in purity and righteousness.
    3. Those that stand before the "Great White Throne" will be bearing their own sins. This is not a time or place to determine guilt or innocence.
    4. "Let the field be joyful, and all that is therein: then shall all the trees of the woods rejoice before the Lord: for He cometh to judge the earth; He shall judge the world with righteousness and the people with His truth." (Psalm 96:12-13)

II. **The Period of Judgment (11)**
    1. Heaven and earth will pass away. There is reverence and awe in heaven.
    2. "*There is no place for them*" – heaven and earth will be gone; and they have no place in heaven.

3. This earth is reserved for fire. (2 Peter 3:7)
4. Isaiah 65:17 reveals there will be a new heaven and a new earth.
5. There will be no place to hide.
6. The masses stand terror-stricken; waiting.

III. The Persons of Judgment (12)
1. Both small and great will be judged.
   A) rich and poor (king, pauper)
   B) educated/uneducated
   C) religious/non-religious
   D) rulers
   E) authority
   F) common
2. The summons will be delivered and all who are unbelievers will be called to court. None will be exempt and there will be no escape.
   A) The sinner will be there. (lived for self)
   B) The self righteous will be there. (works)
   C) The church member will be there. (motions)
   D) The procrastinator will be there. (The road to hell is paved with good intentions.)
3. Satan does not care if you go to hell from the gutter, the pulpit, the pew, the choir, or the Sunday School Class.
4. Persons are in the courtroom not for breaking a law but for rejecting Jesus Christ. (John 3:18)

"Is my name written there
On the page white and fair,
In the book of Thy kingdom
Is my name written there?"
(unknown)

IV. The Procedure of Judgment (12)

1. There is the basis of judgment. The books will be opened. This judgment is certain.
   A) "Therefore having overlooked the times of ignorance, God is now declaring to men that all people everywhere should repent, because He has fixed a day when He will judge the world in righteousness through a Man whom He has appointed, having furnished proof to all men by raising Him from the dead." (Acts 17:30-31)
   B) "And inasmuch as it is appointed for men to die once and after this comes judgment." (Hebrews 9:27)
2. God has recorded every word, action, and every thought.
3. The Book of Life: The books of records will be exact and fair.
4. Secrets are going to be displayed.
   A) "But there is nothing covered up that will not be revealed, and hidden that will not be known. Accordingly, whatever you have said in the dark will be heard in the light, and what you have whispered in the inner rooms will be proclaimed upon the housetops." (Luke 12:2-3)
   B) "But I tell you that every careless word that people speak, they shall give an account for it in the day of judgment." (Matthew 12:36)
   C) "For God will bring every act to judgment, everything which is hidden, whether it is good or evil." (Ecclesiastes 12:14)

V. The Places From Which They Come For Judgment (13)
1. There is the resurrection to judgment; the resurrection of all unbelievers.
2. The Lord will call forth every human body, every element and particle of every unbeliever who has ever lived.
3. They will come from the sea and the ocean depths.
4. They keep coming, millions and millions.

5. Death and hades will give up their dead.
    A) Death: the body, the grave.
    B) Hades: the spirit (jail of departed spirits).
6. No extradition papers will be sent for Jesus will call with great power the unbelievers to appear.
7. "Every one – every man" will be judged according to his works.

VI. The Punishment of The Judgment (14-15)
1. The sentence at this time will be given.
2. The unbelieving will be cast into the lake of fire. This is the second death. Hell is a real place.
3. Judgment is sure. No lawyer will be there to get you off. His judgment is righteous, final, and impartial.
    A) No forgiveness
    B) No mercy, no grace
    C) No salvation at the Great White Throne or after death.
4. "Do not fear those who kill the body but are unable to kill the soul; but rather fear Him who is able to destroy both soul and body in hell." (Matthew 10:28)
5. The spiritual world is one which last forever.
6. The second death – eternally separated from God.
7. People send themselves to hell. (John 3:16-21)
8. The grounds of judgment will be one's relationship to Jesus Christ, the Son of God.

Conclusion:

Evidence is presented: **Luke 12:47-48** (One will be judged by the light they have had. They will be judged for the things they have done and the things they have not done.)

Defense is given: **Matthew 7:21-23** (Excuses will fail.)

<u>Verdict is presented</u>: **Mark 8:38; Matthew 10:33** (If you do not confess Him before men He will not confess you before the Father.)

- No recourse
- No appeal
- No escape
- Eternity without God

Will you face Christ as Judge or Savior? (John 5:22) The judgment of sin fell upon Christ at Calvary. If you refuse Him as Savior the judgment of sin will fall upon you at the Great White Throne.

"And oh, what a weeping and wailing,
As the last were told of their fate;
They cried for the rocks and the mountains,
They prayed, but their prayer was too late."
(Oswald J. Smith; "The Salvation of God")

"There is therefore now no condemnation for those who are in Christ Jesus." (Romans 8:1)
Every life has a sunset.

<u>HEAVEN: A REALITY BEYOND ALL EXPECTATION</u>
<u>REVELATION 21:1-8</u>

As chapter 21 opens the One who sits on the throne is making all things new. This appears to be John's thesis as he writes. All who have rejected Christ along with Satan and his demonic forces have been consigned for all eternity to the lake of fire. What God had prepared and purposed from the beginning of creation is now being regained and renewed. As always, God will bring about His purpose and His desires.

In the beginning verses of Revelation 21 John speaks of a new heaven, a new earth, and a holy city, new Jerusalem. Fifteen times in Revelation 21 and 22 Jerusalem is called a city. The new Jerusalem will be the capital of the new earth which is God's new heaven. This city is like no other city ever imagined by man. Looking across the many countries of the world there have been many cities that have been called and termed magnificent, glamorous, breathtaking, and beautiful. Well, human terminology cannot begin to describe this new Jerusalem.

Listen to Paul's words. "But just as it is written, 'Things which eye has not seen, and ear has not heard, and which have not entered the heart of man, all that God has prepared for those who love Him'." (1 Corinthians 2:9)

I. A New Heaven And New Earth (1)
1. New (*kainos*)
    A) New as to form and quality, refurbish
    B) To renew qualitatively, a freshness
    C) The act of renewing, renovation
2. In Matthew 19:28 Christ spoke of a time of regeneration when He will sit on His glorious throne.

3. "Heaven and earth will pass away, but My words will not pass away." (Matthew 24:35)
4. 2 Peter 3:7, 10-13 states the earth will be purged and cleansed by fire.
5. Isaiah 65:17; Isaiah 66:22
6. In this new heaven and new earth there will be no more sea.
    A) The sea speaks of danger, storms, and separation as we remember John was separated being exiled on the Isle of Patmos.
    B) There is a connotation of wickedness associated with the sea. (The beast came up from the sea.)
7. In the new heaven and new earth there will be no need of water like today. The climate will be totally different as we know it today.
8. Our bodies will also be different in there glorified state.
    A) The blood is about 90% water.
    B) The flesh is about 65% water.
    C) "Now I say this, brethren, that flesh and blood cannot inherit the kingdom of God; nor does the perishable inherit the imperishable." (1 Corinthians 15:50)

II. A New Jerusalem (2)

1. This city is described as the holy city and will be the capital of God's new heaven.
2. Holy (hagios) this city is sacred, pure, blameless, and consecrated.
3. Jesus has been preparing this place for almost 2000 years.
4. John describes it as being like that of a bride adorned (*kosmeo*; arranged, ordered) for her husband.
    A) Betrothal: God pledged His Son to a redeemed people.
    B) Presentation: The Rapture of the church.
    C) Ceremony: Marriage Supper of the Lamb.

D) Consummation: The time of the new heaven and the new earth along with the holy city come down from heaven.

III. A New Fellowship (3)

1. "When all things are subjected to Him, then the Son Himself also will be subjected to the One who subjected all things to Him, so that God may be all in all." (1 Corinthians 15:28)
2. "Or what agreement has the temple of God with idols? For we are the temple of the living God; just as God said, 'I will dwell in them and walk among them; and I will be their God, and they shall be My people'." (2 Corinthians 6:16)
   A) God now dwells in His people.
   B) In heaven He will dwell among His people; in their very presence.
   C) Jesus will be walking with us, in fellowship.
3. There we will experience a fellowship with our Lord that exceeds human imagination and understanding.
4. We will have made a change of address and in our glorified bodies have joy unspeakable.

IV. A New Day (4)

1. "For the Lamb in the center of the throne will be their shepherd, and will guide them to springs of the water of life; and God will wipe every tear from their eyes." (Revelation 7:17)
2. There will be a number of things eliminated in the new heaven and new earth.
   A) No tears: sorrow, sadness, grief
   B) No death
   C) No mourning
   D) No crying
   E) No pain

3. It appears that all of the things associated with death are eliminated in heaven.
4. The results of a fallen creation are done away with.
5. We will experience freedom from the frailties of all human weakness.
6. "For man is born for trouble, as sparks fly upward." (Job 5:7)

V. A New Truth (5-6a)

1. Our Lord always speaks the truth. It is never ending.
2. John is told to write (*grapho*).
    A) To grave
    B) To describe
3. We are told that heaven and earth will pass away but His word will never pass away.
4. In heaven Jesus will continue to reveal new truth to us throughout all eternity.
5. John receives this message to write from the One who sits on the throne.
    A) He is Faithful and True.
    B) He is the Alpha and the Omega.
    C) He is the beginning and the end.
6. He tells John, "It is done."
    A) "It is finished." (John 19:30)
    B) The history of redemption is now complete.
    C) Creation began without sin and now throughout eternity an end to sin has come.

VI. A New Joy (6b-7)

1. The spiritual hunger and thirst for righteousness is completely satisfied.
    A) "Ho! Every one who thirsts, come to the waters, and you who have no money come, buy and eat. Come and but wine and milk without money and without cost. Why do you spend money for what is not bread, and your wages

for what does not satisfy? Listen carefully to Me, and eat what is good, and delight yourself in abundance." (Isaiah 55:1-2)
- B) The woman of Samaria at the well. (John 4)
- C) John 7:37-38
- D) Revelation 22:17
2. Adoption as sons is fully realized regarding those who are overcomers (placed faith in Jesus Christ).
- A) He will be a Father to the saved.
- B) His presence will be the greatest joy experienced.

VII. A New Environment (8)
1. All the unredeemed sinners are excluded from the eternal city.
2. The outcasts are described by John.
- A) Cowards or fearful – They fell away when their faith was challenged.
  - a) Matthew 10:22; 10:32-33
  - b) Matthew 24:13
- B) Unbelieving
  - a) John 5:40
  - b) John 8:24
- C) Abominable
  - a) Titus 1:16
- D) Murderers
  - a) 1 John 3:15
  - b) Revelation 22:15
- E) Immoral persons
  - a) Whoremongers (KJV)
  - b) fornicators (KJV)
  - c) Revelation 22:15
- F) Sorcerers (pharmakos)
  - a) Mind altering drugs

        b)   Revelation 22:15
    G) Idolaters
        a)   Worshipping something or someone other than the One true God.
        b)   Matthew 6:33
        c)   Revelation 22:15
    H) Liars
        a)   Deceivers
        b)   Distorters of the truth
        c)   Revelation 22:15

3. These outcasts suffer for all eternity an eternal hell.
4. The choices people make in this life will determine their future destiny.
5. These are the ones who stood before the Great White Throne. (Revelation 20:11-15)
6. Hell is also the eternal residence of Satan, the beast, and the false prophet.
7. Matthew 25:41 reveals hell is a place that was not created for man but for the devil and his angels.
8. 2 Peter 3:9 states it is not God's will for any to go there.

Conclusion:

According to Revelation 21:7-8, there are only two kinds of people in the world; those who are believers and those who are unbelievers. There are those who are saved and those who are lost. To which do you belong?

<u>**WHAT ABOUT HEAVEN?**</u>
<u>**REVELATION 21 & 22**</u>

Often times something can best be described when negatives are used. In others words, someone can describe to you better what something is not rather than what some- thing is. For instance, when trying to describe heaven one may examine the Scriptures and see what is not present in heaven and by that find great delight and expectation about the heavenly city. Of course, Jesus will be what makes heaven, HEAVEN!

The things that are absent from heaven:
1. There is no more sea. (21:1)
   A) Separation
   B) Storms
2. There is no sanctuary. (21:2-3, 22)
3. There is no sadness. (21:4)
   A) Sickness
   B) sorrow
4. There is no sin (sinners). (21:8)
5. There is no sun, stars, or moon. (21:23)
6. There will be no shadows. (21:25)

The things that are present in heaven:
1. There will be sharing. (21:3)
2. There will be serenity. (21:4)
3. There will be satisfaction. (21:6)
4. There will be sonship. (21:7)
5. There will be sinlessness. (21:8, 27)
6. There will be saints. (21:9)
7. There will be the shekinah glory. (21:22)
8. There will be security and safety. (21:25)
9. There will be service. (22:3)

"By faith Abraham, when he was called, obeyed by going out to a place which he was to receive for an inheritance; and he went out, not knowing where he was going. By faith he lived as an alien in the land of promise, as in a foreign land, dwelling in tents with Isaac and Jacob, fellow heirs of the same promise; for he was looking for the city which has foundations, whose architect and builder is God." (Hebrews 11:8-10)

"For behold, I create new heavens and a new earth; and the former things will not be remembered or come to mind. But be glad and rejoice forever in what I create; for behold, I create Jerusalem for rejoicing and her people for gladness. I will also rejoice in Jerusalem and be glad in My people; and there will no longer be heard in her the voice of weeping and the sound of crying." (Isaiah 65:17-19)

Heaven will be a place in which all things are new. John in Revelation 21 and 22 reveals there are several "new" things that believers will enjoy. Of course, the New Jerusalem is the focus as John describes the Holy City. The New Jerusalem and the bride, the wife of the Lamb are revealed to John. The implication of the Scripture is that the New Jerusalem coming down out of heaven and the bride are one and the same. This should not create a concern for the reader, for even today cities across the world are characterized by the inhabitants of that city. The Holy City not only reflects its people but it also reflects the glory, majesty, and beauty of the Son of God, the Lamb.

I.   The Splendor of The City (21:9-14, 18-21)

   1.   The bride is finally at home in the Holy City, the New Jerusalem.

A) Revelation 19:7-8
B) The Millennium has come to and end, the honeymoon is over **(Revelation 19:11-16).**
C) The bride is a reflection of the city in all of its radiance and glory.
D) It is also the radiant glory of God that illumines the Holy City with the brilliance like that of a diamond (21:11).

2. The gates of the city (21:12-13, 21)
   A) Twelve Gates
      a) Twelve angels at each gate (22:14)
      b) Twelve tribes' names are written on the gates bringing to mind the covenant relationship God has with Israel.
      c) This is also reminiscent of the twelve tribes as they camped around the tabernacle (N S E W).
      d) Each of the twelve gates are made of a single pearl.
   B) This should be a reminder to all that the entrance to heaven was made possible by the suffering of Jesus Christ.

3. The foundation stones (21:14, 19-20)
   A) The city wall consists of twelve beautiful stones that are inscribed with the names of the twelve apostles.
   B) The magnificence and beauty of the varied colors of these precious stones will make up the foundation of the Holy City.
   C) Many of these stones are not familiar to us today.

4. Streets of gold (21:18, 21)
   A) This gold is like transparent glass, clear and pure.
   B) The light of God's glory will stream right through the gold which is like clear glass.

5. Jasper Walls (21:12, 17)
   A) Jasper – The reflection of God's radiant glory.
   B) The walls measure 216 feet thick.

II. The Size of The City (21:15-17)

1. The city is measured with a golden reed or rod.
2. The New Jerusalem is laid out in a square, that being a perfect cube.
3. The length, width, and height of the city are equal, being approximately 1500 miles each.
   A) The city would reach from the northern most part of Maine to the southern part of Florida and then stretch to Colorado.
   B) The city is 2,250,000 square miles.
   C) The total volume of the Holy City would be 3,375,000,000 cubic miles.
   D) The city would be ten (10) times the size of France and 15,000 times larger than London.
   E) If ten (10) billion people occupied the New Jerusalem, each person would have more than 100 square miles of space.
   F) Being that the Holy City is going to be so large can only send one resounding message to man, "There is plenty of room for all who wish to come and live forever with the Lamb of God."
   G) "Do not let your heart be troubled; believe in God, believe also in Me. In My Father's house are many dwelling places; if it were not so, I would have told you; for I go to prepare a place for you." (John 14:1-2)

III. The Shekinah Glory of The City (21:22-26)

1. There will be no temple in the New Jerusalem. (22)
   A) Revelation 21:3
   B) God will dwell "among" His people.
   C) God will no longer dwell or live "in" them.
2. There will be no need for the sun or moon. (21:23; 22:5)

    A)   The glory of God and the Lamb will illumine the New Jerusalem.

    B)   There will be no need for natural or artificial light.

    C)   Isaiah 60:5-6

    D)   "I am the light of the world..." (John 8:12)

3.   The kings of the earth will bring their glory into it (21:24, 26).

4.   Isaiah 60:5-6

5.   There will be no night, but always days.

    A)   The gates are never closed, unbroken access to God will be experienced.

    B)   "Your gates will be open continually; they will not be closed day or night, so that men may bring to you the wealth of the nations, with their kings led in procession." (Isaiah 60:11)

    C)   There will be perfect peace (Isaiah 65:25).

IV. The Saints of The City (21:27-22:5)

1.   New Jerusalem will be a Holy City without sin nor anything that defiles shall come into it.

2.   Revelation 21:8; 22:3, 15

3.   Only those whose names are written in the book of life are found in the Holy City.

4.   The saints will partake of the blessings of the Holy City (Garden of Eden comes to mind).

    A)   The river of the water of life

        a)   This river comes from the throne of God and the Lamb (Revelation 4:2-11).

        b)   God is the source of abundant life.

        c)   John 4:10-15; John 7:37-38

    B)   The tree of life (22:2)

        a)   In Genesis 2:15-17 the tree was forbidden.

        b)   The trees bears twelve kinds of fruit every month.

        c)   The leaves are for the health of the nations.

5. The saints serve God and the Lamb (7:15).
6. The saints see His face, (in His presence face to face).
7. The saints are sealed. What a joy to belong to Jesus.
    A) The saints are His personal possession.
    B) Revelation 3:12; Revelation 14:1

Conclusion:

The Holy City, New Jerusalem is a:

1. Place of permanence (foundations).
2. Place of purity (no sin, no curse).
3. Prepared place (adorned).
4. Perfect place (cube, four square).
5. Protected place (walls, angels at the gate).

In the New Jerusalem John sees no temple, no sun, no sin, and open gates.

Our position today is that we are seated with Christ in heavenly places. It is for that reason that we are to live in light of what is to come. We should live as citizens of the city to which we belong.

LIVING IN LIGHT OF CHRIST'S RETURN
REVELATION 22:6-16

As the Revelation comes to a conclusion one can see the message being repeated as it was stated in chapter one. We are reminded that the prophecy spoken is from God and is validated by His angel. As stated in Revelation 22:8, John is again acknowledged as God's human instrument who penned the Book of the Revelation. Again the reader is told of the blessings that will be his as the words of the book are heeded. The imminent return of Jesus Christ is again in focus as He is identified with the titles of the Alpha and the Omega, the first and the last, the beginning and the end, the root and the descendant of David, and the bright and morning star.

In these final verses of Revelation the nearness of the glorious day of Christ's return is evident. Much emphasis is given to the time being near and the imminent return of Christ. For that reason every Christian should be living in light of His glorious return.

I. **The Priority Revealed (6-7)**
    1. One is to heed the words of the prophecy of the book.
        A) The words are faithful and true.
        B) The words are God-breathed, therefore it is an accurate book.
        C) This truth also encompasses the entire word of God.
    2. What does it mean to heed these words?
        A) *Heed:* (tereo)
        B) Adhere to, follow, be submissive to, walk under the authority of.
    3. "Only be strong and very courageous; be careful to do according to all the law which Moses My servant commanded you; do not turn from it to the right or to the left, so that you may have success wherever you go. This book

of the law shall not depart from your mouth, but you shall meditate on it day and night, so that you may be careful to do according to all that is written in it; for then you will make your way prosperous, and then you will have success." (Joshua 1:7-8)

4. In light of His return we are to walk under the authority of His <u>Word</u> because it is a faithful and true and will bring blessing to our lives.

II. The Praise Required (8-9)
1. John is overcome by the message he has received.
2. Revelation is a book whose focus is Jesus Christ and His glory.
3. John speaks for the first time since chapter one.
4. John, so overwhelmed by the message of the Lord's return falls down at the feet of the angel to worship.
5. Immediately the angel points John back to God's Word and its authority, and tells him to worship God.
6. In light of His soon return we should take every opportunity to <u>worship</u> God.

III. The Profound Revelation (10-11)
1. The Revelation is an open book available to all that they might read and understand.
2. Daniel the prophet was told to seal up the book.
   A) Daniel 8:26
   B) Daniel 12:4-9
3. The message is to be proclaimed in order that people will hear and produce works of obedience.
4. The profound revelation is clear. **(11)**
   A) When Jesus return every man will be exactly as the Second Coming finds him.
   B) There will be no opportunities for change and new choices; character and nature are forever fixed.

C) At His coming man's destiny is settled.
5. Today the cross separates the saint and the sinner.
6. In light of His return we are to be a <u>witness</u> of His saving grace.

IV. The Promised Reward (12-13)

1. Again He emphasizes His return and He brings His reward with Him.
   A) 1 Corinthians 3:10-15
   B) 1 Corinthians 4:1-5
   C) 2 Corinthians 5:10
2. The One who comes with the promised reward is revealed.
   A) Alpha and Omega (A to Z)
      a) Omniscient
      b) Omnipresent
      c) Omnipotent
      d) All sufficient
   B) The first and the last
   C) The beginning and the end
      a) The Eternal God
      b) John 1:1-3
3. In light of His return we are to be at <u>work</u> as faithful stewards.

V. The Provided Redemption (14-15)

1. The seventh and final beatitude of the Revelation is given. (**14**)
2. "*Do His commandments*" is better translated, "those who wash their robes."
3. The finished work of Christ is the emphasis here.
   A) The saints have washed their robes in the blood of Lamb, Jesus Christ.
   B) Christ's death on the cross opens the way into the Holy City.

C) The receiving of Christ gives one the right to the tree of life.

4. There are those that are blessed who partake of the provided redemption and there are those who are refused entrance because of their rejection of the provided redemption. (15)
   A) *Dogs:* vile, unclean, low moral character
   B) *Sorcerers* (pharmakos) – witchcraft, drugs
   C) *Immoral persons* (pornos) – fornicator, whoremonger. (KJV)
   D) *Idolaters* (eidololatres) – turned from God to a devotion and dedication of idolatry, whether open or secretly.

VI. The Proven Revelation (16)

1. Jesus Christ Himself authenticates the message to the church.
2. His Messianic authority is emphasized.
   A) *"Root"* – Christ's deity is shown for He is the source of life, including that of David.
   B) *"Descendant"* – Christ's humanity is stressed.
   C) Jesus is seen as the God-man.
3. The Bright and Morning Star:
   A) The affections of the bride should be stirred when the saints hear this name given.
   B) This speaks of the dawn of a new day when Jesus comes, God's glorious day.
4. In light of His return we are to <u>watch</u> and <u>wait</u>, looking for the blessed hope and glorious appearing of the glory of our great God and Savior, Christ Jesus (Titus 2:13).

Conclusion:

His visible return is as certain as His virgin birth, vicarious life and death, and His victorious resurrection. We can live in light of His return with a hope that is steadfast and sure. In this hope we will not find ourselves disappointed.

THE FINAL WITNESS OF THE SPIRIT
REVELATION 22:17-21

As Revelation concludes it is certainly not difficult to be captured once again by the grace of a loving God. Just as Genesis begins with the loving hand of God upon His creation, so Revelation concludes with God's loving care for those who might still be outside His embrace. God in His love has four concluding messages that one must hear and heed. Obviously one cannot read the Revelation of Jesus Christ and miss the many instances that the invitations, the warnings, and the gospel message go forth. However, because God is not willing for any to perish He closes the message of Revelation with the final witness of the Spirit.

I.   **The Final Invitation (17)**
1.   "Come" (erchomai) - meaning to appear, bring, enter, and be set.
2.   This is the response of the Spirit and the bride once Christ has spoken of Himself as the bright morning star.
3.   We might call this the greatest invitation that has ever been made, that Christ should return.
4.   The invitation of the gospel message is so simple and easy to understand.
     A)   The one who "hears" ought to have as their prayer "Come," referring to the Lord's return.
     B)   The one who is "thirsty" should come and drink.
     A)   John 4 – Jesus at the well offered living water.
     B)   John 7:37-38
     C)   Isaiah 55:1-2
5.   "Let the one who wishes" – The invitation is open to any and all that desire to come.

6. The word "take" suggests the responsibility of the one who hears the invitation.
7. God's gift must be received. He will not force it on anyone.

II. The Final Warning (18-19)
1. The Words of this prophecy are authoritative (1:1; 22:6).
2. The Words of this prophecy are accurate (22:6).
3. The Words of this prophecy are to be applied (1:3; 22:7, 9).
4. This principle is actually true of God's Word in its entirety.
5. It would have been better for a person to have never been born than to tamper with the Word of God.
6. The most attacked book in all of history has been the Word of God and it stills stands.

III. The Final Message (20)
1. Revelation 22:7, 10, 12, 20
2. This is to the Christian one of the greatest assurance in all of Scripture, "Yes I am coming quickly."
   A) Acts 1:11
   B) Titus 2:13
   C) Philippians 4:5
   D) James 5:8
   E) Revelation 1:7; 3:11
3. In the New Testament there are over three hundred references to the Second Coming of Jesus Christ.
4. One out of every twenty five verses speak of His coming again.
5. These are the last recorded words of our Savior in the New Testament which should reveal to all the need to be prepared and ready.

IV. The Final Prayer (20-21)
1. John's prayer is, "Come Lord Jesus…"
2. Do you find yourself in agreement with the aged Apostle?

3. Do you pray, "Thy kingdom come...?" or does the thought of His coming frightened you because you know you are not ready should He return at the midnight hour?
4. Like John, we can be in agreement with his prayer if we are prepared with oil in our lamps.

Conclusion:

As Revelation begins with the message of grace to the churches (**1:4**), so it concludes with grace being extended to all. It was in the mind and heart of God to give the Revelation for the purpose of showing His bond servants those things which must soon take place. God in His grace has allowed His servants to know those things which are to come. For that reason, we are left with no excuse. Rather we find ourselves with a greater responsibility than ever because we have a greater light and a greater understanding. As we worship, watch, and wait, may we be faithful in our witness of the word of God and the testimony of Jesus Christ.

<u>WORKS CITED</u>

Alcorn, Randy. *Heaven*. Wheaton, Ill: Tyndale House Publishers, 2004.

Alpha-Omega Ministries, Inc. *The Preacher's Outline & Sermon Bible, Revelation*, Vol. 13. King, NC: Christian Publishers and Ministries, 1991.

Anderson, C. Scott, Editor. *The New Century Bible, The General Epistles, Revelation*. New York: Oxford University Press, 19??.

Barclay, William. *The Daily Bible Study Series, The The Revelation of John*, Volume 2. Philadelphia, PA: Westminster Press, 1976.

Green, Oliver B. *The Revelation*, Greenville, SC: The Gospel Hour, Inc. 1963.

Jeremiah, David. *Escape The Coming Night*, Study Guide, Vol. 1. San Diego, CA: Turning Point for God, 2001.

______________. *Escape The Coming Night*, Study Guide, Vol. 2. San Diego, CA: Turning Point for God, 2001.

______________. *Escape The Coming Night*, Study Guide, Vol. 3. San Diego, CA: Turning Point for God, 2001.

______________. *Escape The Coming Night*, Study Guide, Vol. 4. San Diego, CA: Turning Point for God, 2001.

Jones, G. H. *The Alliterated Outline of The Bible*. Harare, Zimbabwe: C.M.M.I. Publication, 1988.

King James Version, Holman Verse Reference Jewel Edition, Nashville, TN: Holman Bible Publishers, 1981.

Lahaye, Tim. *Revelation*. Grand Rapids, MI: Zondervan Publishing House, 1973.

MacArthur, Jr. John. *The MacArthur New Testament Commentary, Revelation 1-11*. Chicago, Ill: Moody Press, 1999.

__________. *The MacArthur New Testament Commentary, Revelation 12-22*. Chicago, Ill: Moody Press, 2000.

McGee, J. Vernon. *Thru The Bible*, Vol. 5. Nashville, TN. Thomas Nelson Publishers, 1983.

Phillips, John. *Exploring Revelation*, Grand Rapids, MI: Loizeaux Brothers, 1991.

Sightler, Harold B. *Revelation*, Greenville, SC: Tabernacle Baptist Church, 1982.

Wiersbe, Warren W. *The Bible Exposition Commentary*, Vol. 2. Wheaton, IL: Victor Books, 1989.

Willmington, Harold L. *The Outline Bible*, Wheaton, IL: Tyndale, 1996.

Zodhiates, Th.D., Spiros. *The Hebrew-Greek Study Bible, NASB*. Chattanooga, TN: AMG Publishers, 1990.

ABOUT THE AUTHOR

Dr. Billy J. Owensby is a native of Commerce, Georgia. He is married to Deborah (Poole) Owensby. They have two grown children, Jeremy and Ryan who are both married. Dr. Owensby and his wife Deborah have six grand-children.

Currently Dr. Owensby is the pastor of Union Baptist Church in Hull, Georgia. He has pastored other churches in Louisiana and Northeast Georgia. He is the founder and president of North Georgia Baptist Theological Seminary and S.T.E.P. Ministries (Spiritually Training & Equipping People). Dr. Owensby holds an Associate of Divinity Degree and a BGS Degree from New Orleans Baptist Theological Seminary. He is also a graduate of Bethany Theological Seminary where he earned a Master Degree and he is also a graduate of Louisiana Baptist Theological Seminary from which he earned a Doctor of Ministry.

Other works by the author are:

1. The Expositor's Notes: Selected Sermons
2. The Expositor's Notes: I Timothy
3. The Expositor's Notes: 1-2-3 John (Genuine Christianity)
4. Ephesians: Breaking Down The Walls
5. James: From Belief To Behavior